WHEN THE ROAD GETS ROUGH

WHEN THE ROAD GETS ROUGH

**Ed
Hindson, D. Phil.
and
Walter
Byrd, M.D.**

Fleming H. Revell Company
Old Tappan, New Jersey

Our gratitude and appreciation to Karen Schon and Jeanne Mason, who typed the original manuscripts for this book.

Library of Congress Cataloging-in-Publication Data

Hindson, Edward E.
  When the road gets rough.

  Includes bibliographical references.
  1. Christian life—Biblical teaching.   2. Pastoral counseling.   I. Byrd, Walter, 1949–   . II. Title.
  BS2545.C48H55   1986   248   86-17916
  ISBN 0-8007-1495-4

And we know that all things work together
for good to those who love God, to those who
are the called according to His purpose.

Romans 8:28 NKJV

Contents

7

Introduction

Roads are meant to be traveled, but sometimes they can get pretty rough. Life is such a road. It can lead to excitement and adventure or it can lead to failure and despair. Life is never all joy and no sadness. It is never success without failure or gain without pain. No matter who travels life's paths there will be obstacles to face and pitfalls to avoid.

This book is written to encourage fellow travelers on the rough road of life. The longer you travel life's highway the more you will realize that life is a journey of faith. Martin Luther once said: "We are not yet what we shall be but we are growing toward it, the process is not yet finished but it is going on, this is not the end but it is the road."

No matter how much personal preparation you have made for the journey there will be obstacles ahead about which you never dreamed. Problems will have to be faced and decisions will have to be made. In every crisis of life there will be lessons to be learned and new growth to be attained. In every difficult circumstance you will be faced with the realities of life itself. At each new juncture you will have to decide the direction your life will take. At times there will be others to help you along. But sometimes you will find yourself traveling all alone. Do not despair, for when you need Him most God is there. He will share your heartaches, bear your burdens, and help you find the answers to your problems.

How to Handle Life's Toughest Problems

Everybody has problems! The nature and complexity of those problems may differ, but to the sufferer each is very real. We have spent a lifetime helping people struggle through their problems. We are not experts with simple, pat answers to dab on the deep wounds of life; rather, we are fellow strugglers, ever learning to deal with our own problems while helping others find answers to theirs.

In God's economy there are no experts. While we assume that those with professional credentials have all the answers, God reminds us that He is the One who has the answers. The message of the Bible is one of help for the hurting. In it are the greatest spiritual resources in all the world. We are convinced that, ultimately, God alone can help you deal with your problems.

While the Christian life is one of joy and blessing, it is not a life devoid of problems and troubles. Indeed the Bible reminds us that God comforts us *in* our troubles while not always necessarily removing us *from* our troubles (2 Corinthians 1:4). In fact, suffering and trouble are His methods of shaping our character. The Scripture also reminds us that God is greater than our problems. Since He rules the universe, He overrules every circumstance of life for our own good (Romans 8:28). In our humanity, we want to run from problems, while God wants to use those problems for our own good.

Developing the Right Heart Attitude

Anyone can have problems, but how we handle those problems determines whether they become opportunities for growth or the means of our destruction. Learning to handle life's problems with the right heart attitude honors the Lord and brings His favor and blessing upon our lives. Wrong attitudes express our inner bitterness toward God for allowing problems to come into our lives in the first place. They express our inner frustration with life and our refusal to believe that God is really in control.

We begin conquering our problems when we face them. As long as we deny that we have a problem, we will never really deal with it. Confession is essential to repentance. We must confess (admit) our sins in order to repent (turn) from our sins. Whether we like it or not, most of our problems are the result of sin in our lives. Only when that sin is faced as reality will we take responsibility to correct it. The procedure is simple to understand:

1. Face reality. Stop pretending things are fine when they are not. Denial may make you feel better for a while, but it will not correct your problems.

2. Take responsibility. Deal with your own problems. No one else can solve your problems for you. You must take responsible steps of action to confront your problems and correct them.

3. Do right. There is a right way and a wrong way to handle every problem. God's way is right. Find the right way and do it!

Problems Are Really Opportunities

In relation to the ultimate purposes of God you really don't have any problems! You have opportunities. God allows problems to come into our lives to help us learn to trust Him more. Every time we exercise faith in Him, we are actually growing spiritually. Thus, our problems are really opportunities for spiritual growth. Romans 8:28 promises us that "... all things work together for good to them that love God, to those who are the called according to His purpose" (NKJV). Spiritual maturity is learning to view every problem of life as a new opportunity to experience the good purpose of God in our daily lives.

The key to handling any problem is learning to commit it totally to God. In the face of His own crucifixion, our Lord "... did not threaten, but committed Himself to Him who judges righteously" (1 Peter 2:23 NKJV). That means that Christ Himself had to learn to completely trust God the Father, who is the righteous judge.

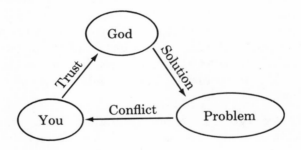

Our ability and willingness to trust God in every circumstance depends upon our confidence in His goodness and His motives. All uncertainty on our part is ultimately distrust of His basic nature and character. The person defeated by his problems is really questioning God's ultimate integrity. If He is really the all-wise and all-loving God, we must learn to trust Him and His Word in the face of any problem.

From God's point of view, you don't have any problems ... just opportunities! You may feel, "I've got a lot of opportunities, then!" It may be that you do. But if you will learn to see them as opportunities, you have made the first real step toward learning to trust God to turn those opportunities into full-fledged *blessings* in your life. If you can trust Him to save you, you can trust Him to help you. His will is to give you all good things (Romans 8:32) and to fill your life with joy (John 15:11).

When the road of life gets rough, God is always there reaching out to help us. When we learn to trust Him and reach out to Him by faith, we find the path easier to walk. Where once we stumbled, now there is progress. Where once we crawled, now we can run. The prophet Isaiah said: "But they that wait upon the Lord shall renew their strength; they shall mount up with wings as eagles; they shall run, and not be weary; and they shall walk, and not faint" (40:31).

1

Anger

Orge, any natural impulse; hence, anger, displeasure. Similar to hatred or enmity (echthra); *the opposite of love* (agape).

Anger can be the most damaging of all emotions. It can make a person say or do things he will regret for a lifetime. Anger can dent a friendship, damage a relationship, or destroy a marriage. Out of control, anger can become the most destructive force in the world. Yet, under proper control and coming from a righteous motive, it can be a powerfully positive force for good.

Anger Is Not Always Sinful

The Greek word for anger is *orge,* meaning "any natural impulse." Anger is the strongest of all passions. The

Bible makes it clear that all anger is not necessarily sinful. In fact the Scripture states that "... God is angry with the wicked every day" (Psalms 7:11). There is much in the Bible about the anger and wrath of God toward sin. God hates sin, but He does not hate it sinfully. Expressions of anger at sinful acts are normal and sometimes even necessary.

The Apostle Paul admonishes us to be angry and sin not (Ephesians 4:26). This injunction clearly shows it is possible to feel righteous indignation over some heinous act of sin. Every decent person becomes angry over the mass murder of innocent people, for example. Nevertheless, it is difficult to limit our anger to righteous indignation. We usually become more indignant than righteous!

Anger May Become Sinful

That is why Paul goes on in this verse to warn us not to let the sun go down upon our wrath, lest we give the devil a place to work in our lives (Ephesians 4:26, 27). When we become angry and stay angry, we ultimately hurt ourselves worse than the original offense did. We make ourselves victims of someone else's sin.

Anger gets out of control when we fail to deal with it properly. It can lead to all sorts of conflicts and offenses. Jesus Himself warned us: "It is impossible but that offences will come" (Luke 17:1). Being a Christian does not give you a spiritual insurance policy against hurt—what you need to learn is how to handle it.

Anger Is Not a Solution

Angry responses usually do not solve problems. They make them worse! When we blow up or clam up because of anger, we are really saying, "Go away. I don't want to deal with you." Thus, sinful anger prevents genuine communication. It builds barriers instead of bridges. Simple ventilation (blowing up) lets everyone know you are angry and will chase them away. On the other hand, internalization (clamming up) does not really hide your .anger and will cause people to avoid you because they sense something is wrong.

There are at least five steps a person can take to deal successfully with an anger-producing situation.

Step 1: Rethink the situation. James tells us, ". . . Let every man be quick to hear, slow to speak, slow to anger" (James 1:19 RSV). Proverbs 25:8 likewise warns us not to embroil ourselves hastily with our neighbor. When you feel anger welling up in your heart, ask yourself, "Have I really been wronged, or am I overreacting?" Evaluate the situation. Remember—appearances can be misleading!

Step 2: Reestablish God's value system. The Bible teaches very clearly that God has a system for establishing the worth of people based on love and acceptance, whereas the world has a system for establishing the worth of people based on competitive hostility. From 1 Corinthians 13, we can draw a clear comparison of these two value systems.

| How God | How the World |
| Values People | Treats People |

1. *Love is patient.* God is understanding of human nature and not only forgives the mistakes of men with great patience, but does not push or rush individuals into changes that are not in their best interest.

1. *Anger has no patience with people.* Anger demands its own way, immediately, and is willing to sacrifice the best interest of other people in pursuit of its own goals. True patience is unknown to the angry person.

2. *Love is kind.* Whereas patience involves the lack

2. *Anger is cruel.* Not only is anger impatient, but

of a nasty reaction to another person, kindness is a positive reaction of reaching out to assist or help another person. It is a positive regard for the needs of others.

anger sees weakness in another person as an opportunity to take advantage of that person. The angry individual sees kindness as an unnecessary weakness.

3. *Love does not envy.* Love does not see another person's success as a threat, and is not uneasy over accolades to another person, whether Christian or non-Christian. The loving person sees his worth as secure in the Lord, and is not jeopardized by the achievements of others. Love genuinely wishes the best for others.

3. *Anger thrives on envy.* The angry person believes that others' success is always to some degree at the expense of his own self-advancement. Therefore he is threatened by the achievements of others, often envious of their accomplishments, and seeks to overtake them by any means possible. He is willing to undermine others in pursuing his own success.

4. *Love does not boast and is not proud.* Love does not believe that it deserves better than it has, and is careful not to be proud of its own achievements at the expense of others. The loving person is truly humble and sincerely cares about others.

4. *Anger has a proud walk.* The angry person sees pride as a weapon with which to intimidate others. Although God has much to say against pride, the angry person uses boasting and the "pride of life" as a ready means to validate his own worth and seek an advantage over others.

5. *Love is not rude.* Love always takes into account the sensitivities of other people. Love understands the temperaments, emotional makeup, and background that make each person unique, deserving of respect and courtesy at all times.

5. *Anger is pushy and often discourteous.* The angry person sees common courtesies and the sensitivities of others as bothersome distractions in his headlong course of self-aggrandizement. The angry person has no real desire to put other people at ease or show genuine concern for their well-being.

6. *Love is not self-seeking.* Love's first purpose in life is not to assure its own success, pleasure, or security. Love honestly and genuinely seeks the good of others. This kind of behavior comes only from the heart of one in whom the Holy Spirit dwells and has active control.

6. *Anger always seeks its own good first.* The angry person sees life as a slugfest whose motto is "To the victor belong the spoils." To the angry person, winning and getting ahead is not everything, it is the *only* thing. Anger feeds the self-centered ambition.

7. *Love is not easily provoked.* Love is patient when it comes to reacting to others emotionally. Love has a flexible and understanding approach to others. It appreciates the need for restraint and calmness in the great majority of life's situations.

7. *Anger is easily provoked by the actions of others.* Anger views impulsive action as both an acceptable and effective means to gain its own ends. "Hair-trigger temper" describes the ease with which an angry person can be provoked. The

Cutting words, petty comments, and divisive rumors are not the by-products of a loving heart.

angry person erupts easily and often.

8. *Love does not bear grudges.* Love understands that forgiveness is the controling force through which God and man are able to have a relationship. Love understands that no relationship can flourish without forgiveness, and certainly there can be no depth in communication.

8. *Anger always remembers an offense.* Bearing grudges, harboring resentment, and taking revenge characterize the chronically angry person's response to the problems and setbacks of life. Not only does anger not overlook a wrong suffered, but rather it engraves a record of the offense on the stone of its heart for permanent remembrance.

9. *Love does not rejoice when it sees people making mistakes.* Love hopes the best for people and is heartbroken when they choose to disobey God. Love never gloats when those who flout God's Word suffer the painful consequences. Loving people are forgiving people.

9. *Anger takes pleasure in the calamity of others.* Anger perceives that those who violate God's Word and therefore experience personal tragedy are "getting what they deserve." While preserving a pious exterior, the angry person secretly hopes others will fall as far away from the Lord as he is.

Step 3: Repent of any unwillingness to forgive. Value the person who has wronged you as worthy of love and acceptance. The Scriptures teach plainly

Because it preserves us from spiritual hardness. It keeps us from thinking that we are alone and unsupported in our struggle.

Move Quickly

"Let not the sun go down upon your wrath" (Ephesians 4:26). The longer you stay angry, the more hardened you will become toward the person who hurt you. When we rebel at the circumstances of life, we are really rebelling against God, since He controls those circumstances. Our attitude is: *I could run the world much better!* The angry man, like the worrier, is attempting the impossible: He is trying to do God's job for Him.

Every Christian is indwelt by the Holy Spirit (Romans 8:9) and has the potential of producing the fruit of the Spirit: love, joy, peace, patience, gentleness, goodness, faith, meekness, and self-control (Galatians 5:22, 23). In the final analysis, there is no excuse for your anger, since God has made every provision for conquering it with loving forgiveness. The Bible's alternative to anger is to "put it away" and replace it with kindness, tenderness, and forgiveness (Ephesians 4:31, 32). In the steps listed above, we have tried to give a series of helpful steps in dealing with the problem of anger. Only active resistance can keep the Spirit from producing fruit. Thus, the angry Christian must face the fact that he is in rebellion against God.

Anger can lead to more sinful attitudes and actions, such as hatred, malice, revenge, blasphemy, and even murder. Like a lighted fuse on a bomb, anger can trigger a multitude of explosive responses. Hatred is a bitter enmity called *echthra* in the Greek. It is the opposite of *agape* (divine love). Malice (from the Latin *malus*— "evil") means a wrongful desire to destroy or harm someone. Revenge (*ekdikeo*) means to hurt someone in return for their hurting you. Blasphemy actually is a

Greek word brought over into the English language, meaning to "speak evil" of someone. Murder (*phoneuo*) begins with anger in the heart (Matthew 5:21, 22).

This progression of evil begins with bitterness and spreads like a plague. Anger is the outward expression of an inward bitterness. It is hatred that, if uncontrolled, can even lead to murder. It is the opposite of genuine love, which forgives and forgets the offenses of others.

Remember, God did not stay angry against you. He loved you in spite of your sin and sent His Son to die for that sin. In so doing, He offers you forgiveness and everlasting life. His is a total and immediate forgiveness. No wonder we who have been so thoroughly forgiven are told to "forgive one another even as God for Christ's sake hath forgiven you" (Ephesians 4:32).

2

Bitterness

Pikria, from a word meaning sharp, keen; hence, bitterness. A deep, long-harbored hurt.

Bitterness is the most dangerous of all attitudes to healthy Christian living. It will eat away the vitality of your spiritual life until your once-vibrant testimony is in shambles. It is the cancer of the soul, claiming millions of victims every year. It spreads faster than the common cold and threatens the survival of many churches. Nevertheless, there is a dynamic cure for this dreadful scourge.

The principle of forgiveness is a truly powerful force in the believer's life. It can melt the hardest heart and clear the most clouded conscience. When used properly, forgiveness paves the way for reconciliation between the worst of enemies. It is often the key to the abundant blessings of God, as it unlocks the soul to the work of the Holy Spirit.

Life Is Full of Hurts

Jesus Himself warned His disciples: "It is impossible but that offences will come" (Luke 17:1). Life is full of hurts, and it always will be! As long as you live, people are going to offend you, hurt you, and disappoint you. But you needn't be the victim of their offenses. You can learn to rise above life's disappointments.

Jesus told His disciples to handle the problem of offenses and bitterness by learning to forgive, and so must we. He said: "Take heed to yourselves: If thy brother trespass against thee, rebuke him; and if he repent, forgive him" (Luke 17:3). Notice that we have two obligations when we are offended. The first is to *rebuke* and the second is to *forgive*. Now, a rebuke is not biting off someone's head. It is a plain statement of truth—"What you said really bothered me." "It hurt me to know you felt that way." Remember, it takes the greatest spiritual maturity to give a rebuke in the right spirit, and to receive one that way, too! The Bible teaches we are to speak "the truth in love" (Ephesians 4:15).

Learning Lessons From Life

Everyday life is often our best teacher. Some of the greatest lessons we can ever learn are from well-intended rebukes we receive from others—especially our friends. However, in order to learn those lessons, we cannot allow ourselves to view a rebuke with hostility.

Jesus put it this way: "And why do you look at the speck that is in your brother's eye, but do not notice the log that is in your own eye?" (Luke 6:41 NAS.) All too often we fail to realize how badly we are behaving. That is why the believer is to rebuke those who offend him, rather than spreading the offense through gossip. We are to go directly to the person who is the source of the offense (Matthew 18:15). Failure to do so may result in the most serious of consequences—God withholding His forgiveness of our own sins! (Matthew 18:33, 35.)

Unity and oneness among Christians is a serious matter with God. He considers a longstanding grudge against another person a major setback in the Christian's life. Christ states in John 17:17–21 that *sanctity* (the Christlikeness of the believer) is largely measurable by how much *oneness* (unity) exists between that believer and others. Considering the importance to God of such oneness among Christians, it would be well to examine the proper way to accept a rebuke from another believer without becoming permanently offended. In the chart below, we can see how taking offense at another Christian usually generates one of four categories of feelings. We tend to feel either disgruntled (angry), disappointed (hurt), deceived (used), or defensive (accused).

Each of these four feelings is based on an underlying idea we have in our minds. In the case of the *disgruntled* (angry) believer, the underlying idea is, "I've been offended." In the case of the *disappointed* believer, the underlying idea is, "I've been betrayed; someone has let me down." The *deceived* beliver thinks, "I've been manipulated, even used." The *defensive* believer's underlying idea is, "I've been potentially threatened or accused without grounds." The defensive believer will sometimes embark on a mini-campaign in his community or church to recruit as many people as possible to his point of view. The diagram on the next page gives an easy-to-read display of the four categories of feelings of the *bitter believer*.

THE FEELING BEING GENERATED	THE UNDERLYING IDEA
I feel disgruntled (angry)	I've been mistreated (abused)
I feel disappointed (hurt)	I've been betrayed (let down)
I feel deceived	I've been manipulated (used)
I feel defensive	I've been threatened (accused)

Underlying all these ideas in the diagram, is insecurity. This insecurity comes from our disbelief that God really cares about our personal needs or that He controls the circumstances of life. The Scriptures teach that God is indeed in control and, therefore, the believer need experience no underlying insecurity when facing the problems and rebukes of life. "And we know that all things work together for good to those who love God, to those who are the called according to His purpose" (Romans 8:28 NKJV). In order to properly deal with the offenses of life and not allow them to turn into bitterness, we must understand the feelings these offenses can generate. We must be aware of the underlying ideas that often accompany such feelings and be able to trace these back to some insecurity in our own lives. This insecurity must be found, defined, and corrected by claiming God's promise that He is at work in our life to produce the best in every conceivable situation.

An Unforgiving Spirit

The Scripture clearly indicates that an unforgiving spirit is the mark of an unconverted soul. Notice the Parable of the Unforgiving Servant (Matthew 18:21–35). Though forgiven a 10,000 talent debt (equivalent to 10 million dollars), he vindictively held a 100 pence debt (less than a dollar) against his fellow servant and came under the wrath of judgment. True Christians are known by their forgiving spirit. Those who have been forgiven much by God ought to be willing to forgive the sins and wrongs done them by others.

Our Lord further told His disciples that if someone offended them seven times a day and repented each time, they should forgive him. To which the apostles said unto the Lord, "Increase our faith" (Luke 17:5). Whereupon, Jesus simply told them that if they had "faith as a grain of mustard seed" (Luke 17:6), they could move trees. In other words, He said: "You don't need more faith—use the little you have."

Seeing Ourselves as God Sees Us

In order to further help His disciples understand the importance of the powerful principle of forgiveness, Jesus shared the parable of the Unprofitable Servants (Luke 17:7–10). In this story, Christ dealt with the disciples' attitudes toward themselves and others. He reminded them that ultimately they were just that—"unprofitable." He wanted them to see themselves as they really were.

Selfish and insecure people get angry. Selfish and insecure people are easily offended. They often try to compensate for this by trying to make people think they are more important than anyone else. They can never figure out why God's world does not revolve around them and their plans. Therefore, they suppose that God doesn't really care for them. They become easily upset when things do not go their way. They never see themselves as God actually sees them. In order to learn to forgive others effectively, we must ultimately see ourselves for what we really are—unprofitable servants, yet immensely and unconditionally loved by God. Only then are we in a proper position for God to work in our lives.

Excuses for Not Forgiving

In our selfishness, we muster a myriad of excuses for not forgiving. These include:

- Revenge   (*I enjoy hating him.*)
- Anger   (*I'm too upset to forgive.*)

- Jealousy   (*I can't let him do this.*)
- Fear   (*I'll be hurt again.*)
- Pride   (*I was right; he was wrong.*)
- Emotion   (*I don't feel like forgiving.*)
- Self-righteousness   (*He doesn't deserve it.*)
- Guilt   (*I can't even forgive myself.*)
- Suffering   (*I'm just too hurt to forgive.*)
- Worry   (*What if he doesn't understand?*)

The ultimate excuse is *I can't forgive,* which really means *I won't forgive!* You can do anything that is right. God always empowers us to do what is right. His grace is always sufficient, no matter how difficult the task. When we forgive others, we confirm what Christ did for us on the Cross when He died for our sins so that we might be forgiven.

Let the Power of God Loose in Your Life!

The Scripture clearly states that wrong attitudes grieve the Holy Spirit and hamper God's work in our lives. Therefore, we are told: "Let all bitterness, and wrath, and anger, and clamour, and evil speaking, be put away from you, with all malice: And be ye kind one to another, tenderhearted, forgiving one another, even as God for Christ's sake hath forgiven you" (Ephesians 4:31, 32).

Often we fail to see our own responsibility in dealing with bitterness. We must put away all wrong feelings that stem from bitterness. The chain reaction of bitterness eventually leads to open and public conflict, which hurts others and damages the cause of Christ. We must learn to forgive others just as completely and totally as God has forgiven us. We must search out those points of insecurity within us that breed erroneous ideas and feelings—feelings that make us quick to take offense.

The powerful, positive principle of forgiveness will unlock your embittered spirit and set the power of God free in your soul. It will make you kind, tenderhearted, and forgiving. It will make you Christlike.

3

Communication

Koinoneo, *to have in common. It is the basis of all true fellowship and leads to unity and cooperation.*

Communication reflects the very nature and character of God Himself. He is the source of all communication. He is the God who speaks and reveals Himself to mankind. In eternity past, the triune God (Father, Son, and Holy Spirit) was in perfect communication with Himself (Genesis 1:26). God did not create man because He was lonely, but because He chose to do so. At first the world was a picture of the beauty of that harmony. God was in perfect communication with Himself, His world, and with man. Man was in perfect harmony with nature. He was in love with his wife, and they were in perfect communication with each other. Their fellowship was unbroken.

Sin Breaks Communication

Adam and Eve were created in God's image and endowed with human intelligence. They had the gift of communicating instantly—with God and with each other. Theirs was a unique relationship of total communication based on total honesty until sin entered and shattered their world. With sin came lying, blaming, anger, hatred, murder, cheating, and so forth. Communication was broken! They hid from the God who loved them (Genesis 3:8). They blamed each other for their sin. And the world has never been the same since.

By our sinful nature, we inhibit communication. We start building *walls* to hide within, instead of building *bridges* to reach out to others. We lie, we hate, we steal, we criticize, we condemn. Yet, the very God that made us has taken infinite pains to communicate His love to us. In the Old Testament He gave us His Law, He sent His prophets to announce His plan, He raised up armies to judge us and heroes to bless us. In the New Testament, He sent His Son from heaven to communicate His love to us. In His Son, God offers us peace, forgiveness, and reconciliation.

Building Bridges or Barriers?

God has built a bridge of communication to us, and we need to learn to build bridges to others. Putting up barriers around your life will cut you off from genuine communication. It will leave you lonely and empty. "But, there are risks involved in building bridges," some will say. Yes, but the rewards are worth the risk! No one wants to be hurt, but clamming up will leave you alienated, isolated from the very people God may intend to be blessings in your life.

Misunderstanding always comes of poor communication. We judge, condemn, and criticize those people and things that we least understand. Out of our own ignorance, we make a situation worse, when God wants us to correct it. Don't be the cause of problems. Learn to become part of the solution!

Five Key Principles

In Ephesians 4, the Apostle Paul gives five keys to effective communication:

1. Stop lying. Start telling the truth. "Wherefore putting away lying, speak every man truth with his neighbour: for we are members one of another" (Ephesians 4:25). People lie to each other every day! "How are you doing?" someone asks. "Oh, I'm fine," is the usual reply. Half the time, at least, that answer is a lie. When someone is upset, another will ask, "What's the matter?" "Nothing!" will come the explosive response. What that answer really means is, "Go away. I don't want to talk about it." Honest communication depends on honest conversation. Telling the truth builds bridges. Lying builds barriers. When people see you are not being honest with them, they will stop talking to you.

2. Stop hating. Start loving. "Be ye angry, and sin not: let not the sun go down upon your wrath: Neither give place to the devil" (Ephesians 4:26, 27). In this passage we are warned not to stay angry, because anger destroys communication. Anger will lead either to aggressive or depressive behavior; it causes us to strike out at others or to put down ourselves. Either way, its destructive force hurts us and those with whom we are angry. When anger comes into your life, deal with it quickly and settle it. Don't let one day pass without eliminating your anger. Otherwise, you are giving Satan a place to defeat you. No one wants to be around an angry person. It drives children away from their parents, and it drives husbands and wives away from each other.

It destroys communication and thereby destroys relationships. By contrast, love forgives, restores, and com-
municates.

   3. Stop stealing. Start giving.   "Let him that stole
steal no more: but rather let him labour, working with
his hands the thing which is good, that he may have to
give to him that needeth" (Ephesians 4:28). Stealers are
takers, selfish by nature. The Apostle Paul reminds us
that we need to stop stealing and develop the grace of
giving. In marriage, some people are takers by nature.
They never learn to give, and their marriage collapses.
Selfish people destroy communication; unselfish people
build communication by building bridges to each other
with gifts of kindness.

   In interpersonal relationships, ask yourself, "Am I a
giver or a taker?" Givers tend to see the worth and importance of other people and therefore are apt to bring
out the best in others. Takers, on the other hand, tend to
see the world solely from their own standpoint. They
provoke others to evade, repress, or deny their inner-
most feelings.

   4. Stop cutting down. Start building up.   "Let no
corrupt communication proceed out of your mouth, but
that which is good to the use of edifying [building up],
that it may minister grace unto the hearers. And grieve
not the holy Spirit of God, whereby ye are sealed unto
the day of redemption" (Ephesians 4:29, 30). Some people excel at cutting down everything and everybody.
This passage warns that such negative communication
grieves the Spirit of God! Your mouth is to be an instru-
ment of God's grace, not a fountain of bitterness and
cursing. Every time you cut someone down, you destroy
communication. You drive people away from God, instead of drawing them closer to Him. What we communicate verbally should encourage and strengthen those
who hear us.

5. Stop overreacting. Start acting like a Christian! "Let all bitterness, and wrath, and anger, and clamour, and evil speaking, be put away from you, with all malice: And be ye kind one to another, tenderhearted, forgiving one another, even as God for Christ's sake hath forgiven you" (Ephesians 4:31, 32).

Here the great apostle warns us not to handle our problems like pagans. Don't blow up! That only makes things worse! Notice the chain reaction in verse 31. We start with bitterness, which soon leads to wrath and anger. That, in turn, leads to clamor (two or more people yelling at each other), which takes us on to evil speaking (literally *blasphemy* or slander), and finally to malice (a deliberate attempt to do someone bodily injury). Such behavior is not of God. It is a worldly response to problems, yes—but not the Christian response. Such overreactions drive people away from us and destroy communication.

One of the most common reasons for Christians overreacting in situations that require skillful communication is a failure to realize just how complex good communication really is. Effective communication can best be thought of as a circular process, made up of at least six components. The diagram below depicts these six components of communication.

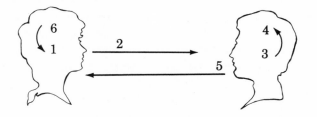

1. What you mean to say.
2. What you actually say.
3. What the other person hears.

4. What the other person thinks he hears.
5. What the other person says about what you say.
6. What you think the other person says about what you said.

From this diagram, it is evident that communication is a complex process. People prone to overreacting when trying to communicate with others may simply misunderstand or overlook the message conveyed in one or more of these six ways. Don't jump to conclusions. Give the other person every opportunity to express himself clearly.

True Christian behavior leads to real communication with others. Only those who have been forgiven can really forgive. We can communicate with one another because God has communicated His love to us.

Develop Communication Skills

There are four skills you can use to convey an attitude of helpfulness and openness, thus making it easier for someone to talk about his or her problem. These can be thought of as four listening skills:

1. Ice breakers.   These are phrases that indicate to the other person your willingness to get involved. Phrases such as "Do you want to talk about it?" or "We need to discuss this, don't we?" convey your interest to the person. Evasive, bored, or dismissive remarks are quickly read by the other person, and real communication becomes impossible.

2. Acknowledgment and positive regard.   Positive regard simply means approaching another person with the frame of mind that they are worthwhile and fully deserving of your attention and concentration. People know when they are being patronized or talked down to. For good communication to occur, both parties must feel accepted as being worthy participants in an open and free discussion based on honesty and positive regard for each other.

3. *Silent listening.* Silent listening simply assures the other person, through your manner, your facial expression, your eyes, and even your breathing, that you are neither bored nor preoccupied, but are fully intent on hearing and understanding what is being said. Averted eyes, covert glances at your watch, occasional sighs, fidgety hands—all these assure the person you have better things to do with your time and he is wasting his time talking to you. Great men throughout history have always understood this—the surest mark of respect is undivided attention.

4. *Active listening.* This refers to the short phrases and interjections we use during the process of communication. They tell the other person: "I understand. I'm interested. Tell me more." Active listening is a difficult skill to learn, because many of us are often absorbed in our own thoughts. When others sense that we are forever "in our own world" and would rather not be disturbed, they shy away from engaging us in meaningful communication. "I see what you mean," "Could you help me understand that a little better?"—phrases like these are a part of effective, active listening. They encourage the other person to continue and deepen quality communication

Try This Survey

The following survey was developed to evaluate the quality of communication within the marriage relationship, but it can also apply to any close interpersonal relationship—at work, at church, or in your neighborhood. Answer *True* or *False* to each question in the survey.

1. _____ It irritates you when your spouse questions your judgment or doesn't readily approve of your solution to a problem.

2. _____ You privately think of yourself as more logical and realistic than your spouse.

3. _____ You rarely give spontaneous compliments to
your spouse, but instead find yourself more
often making comments of a critical nature.

4. _____ You tend to be short with your spouse—you
never say *please* and *thank you* anymore.

5. _____ You and your spouse never sit down to chat,
except about specific problems.

6. _____ You ask your spouse barbed or leading questions when discussing sensitive issues.

7. _____ Often you read the paper or watch TV while
"conversing" with your spouse.

8. _____ You reply with judgments (good or bad, right
or wrong, okay or not okay) when your spouse
asks you about things.

9. _____ Even casual conversations with your spouse
are likely to turn into arguments or disagree-
ments.

10. _____ Your spouse would probably agree that you
tend to cut other people off before they finish
talking.

If you answered *true* to four or more questions, you
are probably doing too much *talking* and not enough
giving. Sometimes we need to *shut up* so the other person can *open up!*

4

Conflict

Eris, **meaning strife or quarrel. Leads to con-***fusion* **(akatastasia)** *and instability.*

Conflict is one of the greatest problems that plagues the Christian Church today. People become divided and divisive over the most petty and unbelievable things.

A certain university professor taught a class on preaching. Weekends he drove down to Georgia, to pastor a small church. One day he came into class a little discouraged and upset. Departing from his lecture, he explained that this small church seated about 150 people and had an aisle running down the middle.

"You will never believe this," he said, "but after being there for several weeks, I've noticed the same people tend to sit on the same side of the church. Though they move around on their side, they never seem to change sides. Finally, this past weekend when I arrived, I asked one of the deacons, 'Why do these people always sit on this side and those people always sit on the other side?' Taking me into the auditorium, he pointed at the carpeting that ran down the aisle and under the pews. I'd never paid much attention to it before, but suddenly I realized there was a seam, where two pieces of carpeting fit together. Then I realized that one side was just a shade lighter blue than the other. The deacon looked at me. 'Preacher,' he said, 'the people who voted for the light shade sit on this side, and the people who voted for the dark shade sit on the other side.' "

Someone in the preacher's class asked, "Well, what are you going to do about it?"

He replied, "I'm going to get a carpenter in there and tear the whole thing out and put in a *red* rug." It turned out nobody liked the red rug, but they finally began to change sides!

Learning to Lean on God

All too often, we let ourselves become divided over the most petty things and claim those things are of concern to God, when, in reality, God isn't concerned about them at all! The Bible makes it clear that God's real concern is for His children—that they love one another and get along with one another. The Bible also teaches that conflict will always be a part of our lives (Luke 17:1). We are warned, however, not to be the *source* of the conflict. All too often we make the situation worse by the selfish manner in which we respond to conflict. Instead of relying on Him, we take the matter into our own hands.

Learn Your Lesson Quickly

God's purpose in allowing problems to come into our lives is far more important than our personal convenience. He often allows us to suffer through interpersonal conflicts for our own good. Conflicts keep us humble, build patience, and develop our spiritual character. However, if we react negatively, we defeat the purpose of the conflict and have to repeat the lesson. If we miss the whole point of this message from God, He will allow more conflict. That is what the Bible means when it says, "God resists the proud, but gives grace to the humble" (James 4:6 NKJV). When we are humbled and teachable before God, He never allows us to be completely defeated. It is then we experience His grace. It is then He reaches down and meets us at the point of our deepest need.

But until then, we often do not even look for the reaching hand of God to meet our needs. We neglect that outpouring of His grace upon our lives day after day. Until we really face the interpersonal conflicts that enter our lives, we will never find the answer to them. God can take the *worst* of conflicts and produce the *best* of results to His glory and to our benefit. We need to grow up spiritually and come to that point of spiritual maturity where we do not let ourselves get defeated by every little problem that comes along.

The chart on page 44 lists causes of conflict and incorrect passive and aggressive responses. It also presents the assertive response as the correct biblical response.

You need to discover God's ultimate purpose behind your interpersonal conflicts and problems. Remember, He is greater than your greatest problem. He can overrule the worst of problems in order to produce the best of results. He knows what your greatest needs are, and He stands ready to meet them. God wants you to develop assertive and positive responses to the conflicts of life.

Cooperate With His Plan

Don't let a conflict stunt your spiritual growth and hinder God's work in your life. Don't let your problem

CHRISTIAN RESPONSE CHART

The Causal Situation	The Passive Response	The Aggressive Response	The Assertive Response
	This is not a biblical response (1 Corinthians 16:13; Colossians 2:5).	*This is not a biblical response* (John 13:35; Romans 12:17).	*This is a biblical response* (1 Peter 5:9; 1 Thessalonians 5:14).
In situations where the Christian encounters major personal trials.	"God cares little for me, or at least He doesn't act like He does."	"People get what they deserve and God is the judge who makes that decision."	"God is just in all He does, but He tempers that justice with mercy and compassion, encouraging us to grow into the likeness of Christ."
In situations where the Christian is the target of unfair or unacceptable actions by others.	"I'll just act like nothing happened, and try to be cheery."	"Try that again and you'll wish you hadn't; don't tread on me!"	"A problem has developed between us, and I know you'll agree that we've got to honestly face it and resolve it as soon as possible."
In situations that call for the Christian to show sensitive compassion toward another person.	"I care only for you and I will not accept myself unless I can make you happy."	"I am not the kind of person who shows the weakness of emotional sensitivity."	"I understand your hurting and needs, and I will respond with compassion and personal strength to help as best I can."
In situations where the Christian must team up with another person to accomplish a task.	"I am willing to completely throw myself into meeting your expectations and I will feel guilty if I don't."	"I expect you to perform up to my expectations and standards. I will accept no less."	"I am responsible for my behavior and will offer you the opportunity to take responsibility for your actions. Together we can effectively serve the Lord."
In situations that require the Christian to show open and vulnerable communication.	"I am unwilling to voice opinions which might upset you, and I will keep nothing private in my life from you."	"I know what is best for you and I will accept you only if you agree with my opinion."	"I value you and your opinions. I will be honest with you and will appreciate your being honest with me as we seek to genuinely communicate."

become so big that it keeps you from the joy of your salvation. Remember that Romans 8:28 still applies to you: "And we know that all things work together for good to those who love God, to those who are the called according to His purpose" (NKJV). God has a wonderful purpose He wants to accomplish in your life, and when you cooperate with that purpose, you will see beautiful results.

The Scripture reminds us that when we were saved, we became heirs of God and joint heirs with Jesus Christ. I receive not only the blessings of His Spirit but whatever else belongs to a son or daughter of the Most High. He does for me what I could never do for myself! It's no wonder, then, that this passage ends by saying, "Who shall separate us from the love of Christ? shall tribulation, or distress, or persecution, or famine, or nakedness, or peril, or sword?" No! Not any of these things! In fact: "In all of these things we are more than conquerors through Him that loved us" (Romans 8:35, 37). The victory has already been won! We need only learn how to appropriate it. We need to choose an assertive response, not an aggressive or passive one, to the conflicts of life. It takes faith to act assertively on the promises of God's Word when dealing with the people, problems, and situations of this life. But God states that His eyes search the world over, seeking to uphold (help) those believers who are willing to take Him at His Word and walk on in faith (2 Chronicles 16:9).

Causes of Conflict

The ultimate cause of all personal conflicts is sin. Whether it is the sin of selfishness, bitterness, greed, or anger, it is still sin, which feeds sinful behaviors and attitudes. *Sinful actions produce conflicts.* Selfishness feeds greed and anger. Bitterness produces jealousy and contempt. Guilt causes fear and paranoia. It works like this:

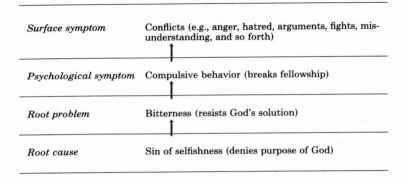

Surface symptom	Conflicts (e.g., anger, hatred, arguments, fights, misunderstanding, and so forth)
Psychological symptom	Compulsive behavior (breaks fellowship)
Root problem	Bitterness (resists God's solution)
Root cause	Sin of selfishness (denies purpose of God)

Doing Things Right

Solving conflicts involves decision making. You must decide that you want to resolve the conflict. Problems rarely go away on their own. We must usually take corrective action in order to eliminate conflicts. Assertive action, based on biblical principles, is necessary if the conflicts are going to be resolved. Learn to tackle every problem God's way. If you will do what is right, He will bless your efforts.

Don't be satisfied with feeble, halfhearted efforts. Remember, the opposite of conflict is fellowship. Only when conflict ceases can fellowship be restored. Don't wait for the other person to come to you. Instead, go to him, lovingly and kindly, to seek reconciliation as soon as possible. Do it today!

5

Death

Thanatophobia, *the fear of death. From dread based upon human fear of death, instead of fear of God.*

The greatest problem in life is death! We naturally fear the unknown, and people fear death more than anything else. We usually fear the death of loved ones more than they do. Even talking about death is difficult for us. We fear that facing the reality of death will make us all too aware of the possibility of our own death, so we try to avoid the subject altogether. Yet, in trying to avoid discussing death, we instill it with such uncertainty and terror that individuals facing it quite often go through five distinct stages before reaching the stage of final acceptance.

The graph below depicts the five stages of death and dying.

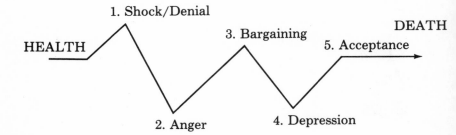

Stage 1: Denial or shock. An individual in this stage often refuses to accept the possibility of his or her own death. Repeated trips to different doctors, endlessly repeated tests (in the hope of better results), refusal to undergo the accepted treatment of a life-threatening ill-ness—all these are symptoms of the denial stage. When facing the reality of their own death, some throw them-selves into frenetic activity, working long hours of over-time or doing endless community-service work. They are trying to deny their own mortality through the whole-sale pursuit of vitality and activity.

Stage 2: Anger. After busily futile attempts to un-dermine the reality of approaching death, people lapse into loneliness, guilt, purposelessness, and a real sense of grievance. This produces the stage of anger—visible anger. It is not uncommon for terminally ill patients to flare up at their physicians, their spouses, their neigh-bors, and relatives—eventually at God Himself.

Stage 3: Bargaining. This is the individual's last effort to escape the now overwhelming reality of oncom-ing death. Large gifts to charitable organizations, vir-tuous promises of a change of life-style, long lists of "New Year's resolutions" are all common to the bar-gaining stage. The length of time spent in this stage de-

pends largely on the patient's ingenuity, energy, and re-
luctance to think about death.

Stage 4: Depression. The person has now moved
past the endless expenditure of energy as seen in the
previous bargaining stage and begins a somber and grad-
ual realization of the consequences of oncoming death.
Friends or companions are especially important in this
stage. Contact with people going through the same experience, participation in terminal patient support groups,
quality counseling—all can minimize the despair of this
fourth stage of death and dying. In many ways, this
stage constitutes a letting go of the fruitless attempt to
walk backwards in time, to a point when death did not
seem to be so real. It is here that secular counseling falls
so dreadfully short.

Stage 5: Acceptance. For many, this stage is hardly
more reassuring or comfortable than any of the others.
For the unsaved individual, acceptance is merely a retreat to a fortress of self-reliance. It encompasses the
hope of extracting a modicum of final purpose and
meaning from the harsh reality of the previous months.
For the Christian, however, the stage of acceptance
brings a renewed appreciation of the fact that death is
merely a transition point, a change of address, if you
will, between life in a physical body on this earth to
eternal life in a spiritual body in heaven. For the Christian facing death, the Bible's message is one of hope and
acceptance.

Accepting the Reality of Death

The Bible reminds us: "It is appointed unto men once
to die" (Hebrews 9:27). Death is inevitable and undesir-
able. It is something to be feared because of what the
Scripture calls the sting (Greek, *kentron*) of death
(1 Corinthians 15:55). The term in the Greek New Testament literally means the "stinger of a scorpion."

Death is not something people casually accept. The Old Testament tells us why people do not want to die. In Ecclesiastes 3:11, the Scripture says God has "set eternity in their heart" (NAS). Man has an innate desire for the eternal and can never fully be satisfied by the temporal aspects of life. From the time we are born, we strive to live forever. We want to know the secret to eternal life, because we who were created in the image of God sense the reality of life after death.

Life After Death

The Bible clearly teaches life after death, for both the saved and the unsaved. To the born-again believer, the Scripture declares: "to be absent from the body is to be present with the Lord" (*see* 2 Corinthians 5:8), and to the unsaved it warns: "many of them that sleep in the dust of the earth shall awake ... some to shame and everlasting contempt" (Daniel 12:2).

The Bible emphasizes that physical death is not the end of human existence. Man enters a conscious eternity, where he faces the possibility of heaven or hell. We make our choice on this side of the grave for either eternal blessing in God's presence or condemnation and exclusion from His presence.

Sometimes we fear death because we get our focus off the eternal and onto the temporal. If you spend your entire lifetime living for the things of this world, you are going to be greatly disappointed, for real life does not consist of the things a person accumulates. Real life is a dynamic fellowship with the living God. If we keep our spiritual focus on eternity, we have every reason to hope and rejoice. The Apostle Paul wrote: "Behold, I shew you a mystery; We shall not all sleep [die], but we shall all be changed, in a moment, in the twinkling of an eye, at the last trump: for the trumpet shall sound, and the dead shall be raised incorruptible, and we shall be changed. For this corruptible must put on incorruption, and this mortal must put on immortality" (1 Corinthians 15:51–53).

The Hope of the Resurrection

Christians have a totally different view of death, because they alone know the One who has conquered death itself. "Death is swallowed up" in the victorious resurrection of Jesus Christ (1 Corinthians 15:54). Thus the beloved apostle asks the ultimate questions: "O death, where is thy sting? O grave, where is thy victory?" (1 Corinthians 15:55.) The reality of death is still there for every one of us, but the sting is gone! God will triumph over death because Christ has already risen for us. "Dust to dust" and "ashes to ashes" holds true only for a while; it is not the final chapter. Far more than that, the Bible declares that though the body perish in the dust, your soul will live forever and stand before God on the day of judgment to be received into heaven.

The hope of the resurrection is the reason Paul could say with triumph: "For to me to live is Christ, and to die is gain" (Philippians 1:21). For the apostle, every day was a new and exciting encounter with the risen Christ and death was but the means of ushering him into the presence of the Savior. Therefore, Paul feared neither life (with all of its complexities) nor death (with all of its uncertainty). To the Christian, death is not something to be feared: It is the first step of a grand entrance into eternal joy and blessing.

Everlasting Life

Death is one of the most feared experiences of life. To the unsaved, it is the ultimate defeat of the human spirit. Man's desire to stay alive is ever threatened by the approaching steps of death. We were born to die. What happens in between our birth and death is the sum and substance of life.

For the Christian who knows the eternal God, death is

only a change of scene, not a change of life. The Scripture states: "He that hath the Son, hath life . . ." (1 John 5:12). One does not have to die and go to heaven to obtain everlasting life. When you were saved, you became a "partaker of the divine nature" (2 Peter 1:4). You already *have* eternal life right now! Learn to live like it! Live above the petty human fears of death and aging, recognizing that the eternal God lives within your soul. When you were born again (1 Peter 1:23), your life became coeternal with the life of God. You shall live as long as God shall live. Why should I be afraid to die? I have everlasting life in my soul! Why should I fear the sting of death? God has called me to live forever. My life is coeternal with His own.

The greatest joy in life is serving the eternal God who is the lover of your soul. The greatest fulfillment you will ever find will be in living for Him and cooperating with His eternal plan and purpose for your life. Stop fearing that which God has already conquered. Learn to have confidence in the character and nature of God. Where is the sting of death? It was drawn by the death of Jesus Christ, who put death to death for everyone who trusts Him as their personal Savior!

6

Depression

Exaporeomai, to find no way through, to be wholly at a loss.

Depression is a common experience to most people at some point in their lives. Physical illness, loss of a loved one, the sense one has "failed in life" may all lead to depression. One out of twenty Americans is diagnosed as being clinically depressed. Even great men of God became depressed for significant periods of their lives: Job, Moses, and Elijah all at some point wished they would die. David became deeply depressed over his sin, and Jeremiah grieved for the sins of his people, Israel.

A depressed person may suffer more real pain than a person with a physical illness. One of the most depressing things about depression is the realization that there is usually no physical cause for it. We should be careful to note, however, that certain physical conditions (such as a chemical imbalance, menopausal change, or hypoglycemia) may cause depression as a side effect. On the other hand, it is equally dangerous to minimize the symptoms of depression. Pretending that nothing is bothering you will *not* cause your depression to go away.

Physical Causes

Depression is sometimes caused by physical conditions that are unrelated to spiritual problems. Any disruption of the physical processes of the brain can lead to chemical imbalances within the nervous system, causing depression. The brain relies on several key chemical substances (neurotransmitters) to maintain a stable level of mood. Imbalance of these neurotransmitters can lead to drastic mood swings and depression.

Other physical causes of depression include: hypoglycemia (low blood sugar); hypothyroidism; endocrine hormone imbalances in blood levels of estrogen or adrenalin; viral infections, such as the flu or mononucleosis; vitamin shortages; drug misuse; exposure to industrial poisons; fatigue; and premenstrual syndrome (PMS). One's spiritual condition alone cannot overcome physically caused depression. These factors must be diagnosed and treated by a qualified physician or psychiatrist. Check with your doctor first.

A Spiritual Problem

Most depression has a spiritual (and psychological) cause rather than a physical one. Depression is most serious among the divorced, the widowed, the unemployed, the guilty, the lonely, the empty. Loss of meaningfulness to one's self and to others always causes serious depression. Lack of self-worth, lack of feeling essential to others, and a lack of intimacy with God may all contribute to one's becoming depressed. Since God is the "God of all comfort," literally, "encouragement" (2 Corinthians 1:3), He is the only source of victory over depression. Whether we want to admit it or not, nonbiological depression is a spiritual problem.

Spiritual Cause of Depression

Look at the unhappy sequence of events that unfolds in the development of a depression brought on by a spiritual crisis of unconfessed and persistent sin in the life of the believer.

Sin

The breaking of fellowship between God and man is the most devastating aspect of sin. Sin is a choice contrary to God's biblical commands in pursuit of our own wants. The outcome of a willful refusal to obey God is that we will reap painful consequences (Hosea 8:7).

Anxiety

The Scriptures teach that sin not only causes a separation between God and man (Psalms 66:18), but sin causes anxiety in the heart of the believer. ". . . I am full of anxiety because of my sin" (Psalms 38:18 NAS).

Confession and restoration of our relationship with the Lord can be one choice we make when we find ourselves under the anxiety caused by sin. "He who conceals his transgressions will not prosper, But he who confesses and forsakes them will find compassion" (Proverbs 28:13 NAS).

Depression   Denial of the sin at hand, and a refusal to
     ↓   confess it and make it right with God,
                    now tumbles the Christian into real de-
                    pression. Psalms 39:2 says that when we
                    keep silent about our sin, the sorrow
                    grows worse.

Despair   Once depression is a continuous part of
     ↓   our existence, then the sadness of the
                    heart can lead to brokenness (despair) of
                    the very will to live. ". . . But when the
                    heart is sad, the spirit is broken" (Prov-
                    erbs 15:13 NAS).

Breakdown   The final state of this process is a break-
                    down of the fabric of the personality, re-
                    ferred to in Scripture as a "drying up of
                    the bones," and sometimes popularly
                    known as a nervous breakdown. "The
                    spirit of a man can endure his [physical]
                    sickness, but a broken spirit who can
                    bear?" (Proverbs 18:14 NAS.)

Depression may be fueled by circumstances far beyond our control, but depression is the end result of not
handling our problems scripturally. For example, the
Bible reminds us: "Be careful [anxious or worried] for
nothing; but in every thing by prayer and supplication
with thanksgiving let your requests be made known unto
God. And the peace of God, which passeth all understanding, shall keep your hearts and minds through
Christ Jesus" (Philippians 4:6, 7).

The passage makes it clear that worry and anxiety
come from a lack of prayer. Most counselees insist that
they have prayed about their problems, but the counseling process reveals that they have not really communicated with God at all. Muttering our frustrations to God
is not really praying! God makes Himself accessible to us

for guidance because He wants us to take action against the problems and discouragements of life.

Physical and Emotional Side Effects

The spiritual conflict that underlies a person's depression will always come to the surface with definite physical and emotional consequences:

- *Hopelessness*
- *Fear of the future*
- *Worry*
- *Pessimism*
- *Irritability*
- *Inability to concentrate*
- *Fear of dying*
- *Fear of change*
- *Lack of confidence*
- *Constant headaches*
- *Loss of sex drive*
- *Withdrawal from people*

In essence, depression is a form of self-pity. It is a self-inflicted means of escape from responsibility in the real world. Something about your world is not quite right, and that bothers you. Eventually discouragement gives way to depression. What initially bothers you could be anything: health, family situation, job conditions, inadequate future security, fear of growing older, and so forth. It is not *what* is bothering you that is so important, as *how* you are handling it. Whenever we become discouraged, defeated, or embittered by our circumstances, we are really questioning God's sovereign control over those circumstances. *How can He really be in control,* we think to ourselves, *and let this happen to me?* Our problem is that we have a self-centered view of the world.

Self-centeredness Leads to Self-destruction

The major cause of suicide is depression. Once a person views the world from a self-centered perspective and concludes that things just are not going to go his way, he may want to escape from that world. As a result, one person commits suicide every twenty minutes in the United States alone! There are seven suicides listed in the Bible (Abimelech, Samson, Saul, Saul's armor-bearer, Ahithophel, Zimri, Judas Iscariot), and all of them were the result of sinful actions.

Sometimes people commit emotional suicide instead of physical suicide. They cut off all their emotional feelings toward God and people. They withdraw into their own inner closet and shut the door of their life. Sometimes this can lead to what psychiatrists call a *psychotic depression,* where the person altogether loses touch with reality. God wants you to open the door and get out of the closet! God wants you emotionally healthy!

Depression does not need to defeat you or destroy you. It can actually become God's tool to discipline you into correcting wrong thinking and wrong behavior in your life. According to Romans 8:28, ". . . all things work together for good to them that love God, to them who are the called according to his purpose." Even depression can ultimately produce good results in your life, if you will allow God to use it properly. He made us with the capacity for depression. However, He did not intend it to defeat us, but to correct us. If we sinfully resist God's purpose in our lives, we are especially vulnerable to serious depression. "But I can't help it," you say. "I don't want to feel this way." You may not want to suffer the consequences of depression, but you will not be able to overcome a depression by simply wanting, wishing, or praying it away. You will need to move out in faith along a road of positive action.

Overcoming Depression

Depression always leads to lethargy and hopelessness. When you are depressed, you feel disinclined to do anything about it (usually because you are not really sure what to do). Yet, you *must take action!*

1. Believe that God is greater than your problems. Whatever circumstances have you down, it is not the end of the world. Look up—God can help you.

2. Turn all those problems over to Him in prayer. Do not just say words—communicate with God (take thirty to sixty minutes). Pray specifically, listing each area of concern. Don't pray that God will take each problem away, but instead pray that He will give you a means to really understand the problem, a mental picture of how to attack the problem a small piece at a time. Follow this daily with a short plan of action and a prayer for the courage to take just one step forward in faith against the problem that day.

3. Believe that God has a purpose for your difficult circumstances. What is He trying to accomplish in your life through these circumstances? How are you resisting Him? Seek out a trusted Christian pastor, trained counselor, or mature friend for an objective opinion on your situation and how you are responding to it (Proverbs 11:14).

4. Recognize that depression feeds on self-pity which must be confessed and forsaken as sin. Do not just patch things up on the surface. Deal with your deeper problem of a poor self-image. Squarely face your self-centered attitude and confess it as sin. The opposite of depression is joy. Thus, the Scripture reminds us: ". . . the joy of the Lord is your strength" (Nehemiah 8:10). When joy is missing, your strength is gone!

5. Realize that you cannot always have your own way. Submission to life's circumstances is really submission to God's will for your life. Frustration and anxiety never solve anything. Remember the truth of 1 Corinthians 10:13, "There hath no temptation taken you but such as is common to man: but God is faithful, who will not suffer you to be tempted above that ye are able; but will with the temptation also make a way to escape, that ye may be able to bear it."

6. Acknowledge you have no valid excuse for staying depressed. Determine to do everything necessary to conquer it! Stop pampering yourself, and start living for others. God will not put more *on* you than He will put *in* you to bear it up.

7. Get up, get out—face reality. God is alive and at work in your life. Remember, sinful thinking (*God doesn't love me; He can't help me*) is just as harmful as sinful behavior. Wrong actions produce wrong feelings. But, wrong thinking also produces wrong feelings. Remember, you are a child of God. Act like it!

8. Avoid major stress. Some of the tension-producing stresses in life can be minimized. Avoid too many major changes all at once. For example, buying a home, changing careers, and having a baby all in one year may crack your nerves. A change of pace in what we do from day to day can also help relieve the minor stresses of life. Too much of any activity, whether study, work, or housekeeping, can get you down. Take a genuine break, do something you enjoy, go somewhere different. There's always a way to make time to treat yourself to something you truly enjoy.

9. Get some exercise. Being "good and tired" from vigorous physical exercise helps you relax, helps you sleep, improves your appearance, and gives you the satisfaction of feeling physically fit. It's best to make exercise a regular part of your daily routine, and recent medical research indicates that regular exercise may actually result in biochemical changes within the brain, which tend to help offset depression.

10. *Confess and forsake sinful actions and sinful thinking.* Think scripturally, like a real Christian— then act like one. Stop making excuses and start making some changes.

11. *Get your priorities in proper order.* Put God first, not yourself. Stop trying to make everything revolve around you and your problems. From a truly Christian perspective, you have no real problems. Instead, you have lots of opportunities to trust your heavenly Father and see Him work in your life.

12. *Get involved with the needs of somebody else.* Get your eyes off yourself and back onto the needs of others. You cease being a missionary when you become a mission field. Remember, Jesus Christ has already commissioned you to go to others. *Christ*-centered thinking is not morbidly self-centered thinking. Positive Christian thinking is God-conscious, not problem-conscious.

Joy Is the Remedy!

Remember, the opposite of depression is joy. The Bible tells us that joy is a fruit of the Spirit (Galatians 5:22). Therefore, the solution to depression is spiritual in nature. The depressed person has become the victim of his feelings. When we feel slighted or neglected, depression sets in. Remember, God is greater than your feelings. He is the source of real joy. Let Him fill the void and restore the joy of your salvation. "A merry heart doeth good like a medicine . . ." (Proverbs 17:22).

7

Divorce

**Apoluo, *to loose from, or send away. Similar to*
aphienai, *to release or separate permanently.***

Every year in the United States, one million marriages
end in divorce. Each day two thousand teenagers must
choose which parent they want to live with. Although
parents are often hurt by their married children's decision to divorce, and embittered couples do such harm to
each other that they never fully recover, it is the children of divorce who suffer most from a conflict they cannot fully understand.

Divorce: Our National Crisis

Recent psychological studies have revealed the devastating effects of divorce upon children. Hurt, confusion,

alienation, and bitterness are only a few of the deep scars left upon the children of a broken marriage. Millions of American children live with the harsh realities of divorce, and millions more are threatened by the ever-impending possibility of parents separating.

"But what about the awful results of keeping a bad marriage together?" someone will always ask. In reality, there is no such thing as a bad marriage. Rather, there are badly behaving marriage partners. Marriage is a partnership, a relationship. When the partnership goes sour, it is because people have gone sour; when we fail to relate properly to each other, the marriage suffers.

What the Bible Teaches

The Bible speaks very directly to the issue of marriage, separation, and divorce, and answers some of life's toughest questions: "What should I do if I am separated? Is divorce always wrong? What about remarriage? Can God forgive me for a divorce?"

Marriage is God's institution. The Scripture clearly states that God Himself ordained marriage before the fall (Genesis 2:20–25). God has also revealed His plan of order for the family (Ephesians 5:22–33). Marriage is a divinely ordained institution and is intended to be permanent. Thus, Jesus said: "For this cause shall a man leave his father and mother, and cleave to his wife; And they twain shall be one flesh. . . . What therefore God hath joined together, let not man put asunder" (Mark 10:7–9). God intended marriages to last, but they can only survive when both partners want them to survive.

Divorce is the invention of man. Nowhere in Scripture does God ever order divorce. However, He does permit it after the fall ". . . because of the hardness of your hearts . . ." (Matthew 19:8). In the Old Testament, divorce was permitted because of moral uncleanness (Deuteronomy 24:1–4). While some have tried to limit this passage to the divorcing of Jewish engagements only, the context

clearly indicates that it is to be applied to the divorcing
of a marriage, as well. In the Law of Moses, remarriage
of divorced persons was allowed (though not necessarily
encouraged). However, remarriage to one's former partner was clearly disallowed, even in the case of the death
of the second partner (Deuteronomy 24:4). God regu-
lated divorce, not because He encouraged it, but because
hardhearted people were sinning against each other and
breaking their marriage vows.

Permission is not promotion. Jesus dealt severely with
the matter of divorce because first-century Jews inter-
preted Moses' permission as an open promotion of
divorce for any reason at all. Thus, our Lord said, "Whosoever shall put away his wife, saving for the cause of
fornication [*porneia,* sexual sin], causeth her to commit
adultery: and whosoever shall marry her that is divorced
committeth adultery" (Matthew 5:32). Thus, He
changed the penalty for adultery from death to divorce.
Even then, He offered forgiveness to the woman taken in
adultery (John 8:1–11) and to the five times divorced
adulteress of Samaria (John 4:3–42).

Marriage is meant to last. The institution of marriage
is God's method of stabilizing a sinful society. The family unit is still the basis of our culture, so when the family fails, society and our culture suffer. God wants your
family to succeed. He has given every encouragement in
Scripture for the family. He even promises "righteousness unto children's children" if we obey His command-
ments (Psalms 103:17, 18). Your marriage can survive.
Don't take the easy way out. Be willing to make it
work.

When a Separation Occurs

The ideal of Scripture is clearly stated in 1 Corinthians 7:10, ". . . Let not the wife depart from her husband."
In other words, couples should not separate. Separa-

tions are harmful and hurtful. They leave both partners susceptible to temptation, and they often cause couples to lose all hope of resolving their conflicts. However, there are times when separation becomes unavoidable because of physical or moral harm. Therefore, this same passage states: "But and if she depart, let her remain unmarried, or be reconciled to her husband: and let not the husband put away [divorce] his wife" (v. 11).

This passage reveals three definite guidelines for separated couples:

1. The separated person is not to establish remarriage as a goal of the separation. Hence, in our present culture, Paul's "let her remain unmarried" must ultimately mean do not date. Nothing will hinder a potential reconciliation more than becoming romantically involved with someone else.

2. The separated couple is to establish reconciliation as their primary goal. Thus, the task of every Christian counselor is to help that couple rebuild their marriage in order to prepare for reunion. He must never give up on people, even when they have given up on themselves. It is important to hold out for the possibility of total reconciliation at all times.

3. The other partner should not seek a divorce to legally end the marriage. Thus, the Scripture places a greater responsibility upon the divorcer than the divorcee (Matthew 5:32; Mark 10:11). It is the one who insists upon the divorce who bears the greater guilt. The divorcer is held responsible for his sin and his partner's potential subsequent sin.

When Divorce Occurs

Many people find themselves the victim of a divorce they never wanted. The Bible clearly commands the Christian to remain with an unbelieving mate as a sanc-

tifying influence upon his or her unsaved partner
(1 Corinthians 7:12–14).

1. Desertion by an unsaved partner. However,
the Scripture also states: "If the unbelieving depart, let
him depart. A brother or sister is not under bondage in
such cases" (v. 15). While a divorce is usually caused by
the behavior of both husband and wife, the Bible indicates that sometimes the actual divorce is the result of
one party's provocation. The Scripture definitely states
that the believer who is the victim of an unbelieving
partner's action is free from the bond of that marriage.
The Apostle Paul then indicates that if the partner
"loosed" in this manner remarries, they have not sinned
(v. 27, 28), but may have "trouble in the flesh." They are
free to remarry, but may still suffer the scars of the previous marriage. Just because you are free to remarry
does not mean you are ready to remarry.

2. Adultery by one or both partners. In the case
of adultery, the Bible clearly teaches that divorce is per-
missible, since the marriage vow has been broken and
the union violated (Matthew 5:27–32). Yet, the Scripture is filled with examples of reconciliation, even after
repeated failure. It is clear that adultery does not have
to mean the end of a marriage. However, merely going
back together and trying to make it work is not enough;
there must be a total recommitment to the marriage
bond by both parties.

Marriage is a covenant relationship between a man
and a woman. When adultery occurs, that covenant is
broken. Therefore, the covenant must be reestablished
and the vow recommitted in order to invoke God's
blessing on the marriage again. Personal forgiveness
should be followed by a formal retaking of the marriage
vow, which will officially mark a new beginning for the
couple.

3. Sinful remarriage. Even when a person has wrongfully, sinfully (unscripturally) divorced and suffers the consequences of that divorce, he or she is still not beyond the possibility of God's forgiveness. There is only one unpardonable sin, and it is not divorce! Therefore, even the sin of divorce can be forgiven. That forgiveness does not excuse divorce; its consequences, even when forgiven, are usually lifelong in their effect.

God's plan for the family is one man for one woman for one lifetime. We must always strive for that ideal as couples and servants of Jesus Christ. Our own marriages ought to reflect the love of Christ for His bride, the Church. We must pledge ourselves to learn to love each other, even as Christ loved us with an everlasting love.

How to Prevent Divorce

Divorce is a "decision" that is totally preventable. Of course, because man has a sinful nature, divorce will be a reality until the return of Christ. However, there are ways to minimize the confusion, miscommunication, insensitivity, and divisiveness that so often lead to divorce. The sensitivity survey below is designed to help improve the quality of communication within the marriage relationship by helping you check your sensitivity to your mate's needs and helping you gather new and meaningful information from your mate's responses.

Marriage Sensitivity Survey

1. What are two things my mate does (or I wish my mate would do) that please me?
   A. _____
   B. _____
2. What are two things I know that I do or could do which please my spouse?
   A. _____
   B. _____

3. What are two qualities in my mate that I admire?
   A. _____
   B. _____
4. What are two things my spouse does that upset or ir-
   ritate me?
   A. _____
   B. _____
5. What single change in my spouse's behavior would I
   like to see in the next two weeks?

   _____

6. What change in my behavior do I think my spouse
   would like to see in the next two weeks?

   _____

This marriage sensitivity survey is a simple, effective
way to take a reading on the quality of communication
in your marriage. This survey is designed to be done frequently by each spouse and then discussed together at a
convenient, quiet time. We recommend giving adequate
time for a good discussion of the responses and praying
beforehand that God will give both of you an open,
teachable, and nondefensive attitude. By taking a few
precautionary measures, such as understanding and im-
proving the quality of communication in marriage, divorce can be prevented.

1. Be honest with each other. Stop pretending
everything is fine if it is not. Your partner can never
make the changes necessary to a happy marriage unless
he/she knows you are unhappy.

2. Be fair with each other. Stop complaining
about the little things. They are only a symptom of
deeper frustrations. Get to the heart of the problem, and
let your partner do the same with you.

3. Be firm with each other. Get tough! Don't give
up on each other; that only proves how weak your love
is. Show how much you care by making every effort to
love and understand each other.

4. Make time for each other. Today's dreams are tomorrow's realities. Start dreaming together. Make plans for special times together, and don't let anything interfere. Increase your love by spending time together.

5. Talk to each other. Learn to listen with your heart. Open up to each other. Self-disclosure will lead to a more intimate relationship.

6. Love each other. Don't take sex for granted. Don't let it get stale and routine. Make time to make love; don't wait until you're too tired. Halfhearted sex will kill a marriage, and neglect will leave you vulnerable to temptation.

7. Forgive each other. Failure is a part of life. There will be times when you fail each other. Learn to forgive and put your mistakes behind you. If you can't forgive together, you can't live together.

Living With a Divorce

A divorce is the end of a marriage, but it is not the end of the world. Your life must go on after divorce. Living with the consequences of divorce will not be easy. Guilt, rejection, fear, failure, and anger are all expressions of the agony of divorce. While there is no excuse for divorce, except our hardheartedness, many have to learn to live with the consequences of a divorce they never wanted. Even when you hurt the most, God has not abandoned you. He still loves you and He still cares (Romans 8:35–39).

If you are now living as a divorced single parent, determine to be the best parent you possibly can be to your children.

Failure

Ekleipo, *to fail, give up, or fall short of attainment. Opposite of succeed.*

Everyone fails sooner or later! Failure is a normal part of human life. It is something we all experience and all need to learn how to handle. If we do not deal with failure properly, we will only get bitter and fail again. Human nature is such that when we fail at something, we immediately look for somebody to blame. When Adam sinned in the garden, he blamed both God and Eve for his failure (Genesis 3:12). When Saul failed to fully obey God's instructions, he blamed his sin on the people of Israel (1 Samuel 15:20-22).

The Bible is filled with examples of human failure.

Adam condemned the entire human race, yet he was the first person to be saved. Abraham was guilty of lying, adultery, and laughing at God, yet he is remembered as the father of the faithful. Jacob deceived people most of his life, yet became the father of the twelve tribes of Israel. Moses never made it to the promised land, yet he was Israel's greatest leader. Aaron succumbed to idolatry, yet he became God's high priest. Samson fell to Delilah, yet he was Israel's greatest warrior. David committed adultery and murder, yet he was Israel's greatest king. Peter violently denied the Lord, yet he was God's spokesman at Pentecost.

Failure Is Not the End!

The first key to growing through failure is seeing it as a universal part of being human and then accepting responsibility for the outcome of your actions. God wants us to learn from failure. We especially need to learn how not to make the same mistake again. We need to face our weaknesses. Whatever can be changed, needs to be changed; wherever we can improve, we need to improve.

If you cannot succeed in a certain area of life, it obviously is not the will of God for you to pursue that area. You might love to play football, but if you do not have the physical ability to play professionally, then God did not call you to be a wide receiver in the NFL! You may enjoy singing but not have the kind of voice that ought to be recorded. Don't spend your life feeling like a failure because you could not succeed at something you were never called to do.

On the other hand, there are things you can do. But, if because of some initial failure you go away discouraged, angry, and upset, then you will never accomplish what you could have, had you just kept trying.

What Is Your Definition of Success?

In order to address the problem of failure, we have to start with a question about success. Does God really want us to be successful? Some of the ultrapious types like to say, "Oh, the Lord really didn't intend us to be successful. We can be failures to the glory of God. The more everything goes wrong, the more spiritual we become." On the other hand, there are those who are bent on success at any cost. Their attitude is—do whatever you have to do to succeed, whether it's biblical or not. "After all," they rationalize, "God wants us to be successful. He doesn't need any more failures."

What is success according to the Word of God? Read Joshua 1:8: "This book of the law shall not depart out of thy mouth but thou shalt meditate therein day and night, that thou mayest observe to do [practice] according to all that is written therein: for then thou shalt make thy way prosperous, and then thou shalt have good success." By this definition, *success is doing the will of God.* There may be things we can do for God that we think should satisfy God in some way, but everything we do for God needs to be done according to the Word of God in order for it to be done in the will of God.

By some standards, Abraham was a total failure. Leaving Ur, the greatest city of his day, he went out to the middle of nowhere to the land of Canaan and there lived and died in obscurity. Yet he is one of the most illustrious men who ever lived. Moses led the slaves of Israel out of Egypt into a wilderness and was never personally guided into the promised land. He died a failure by modern standards, yet he is one of the greatest men God ever used. Christ Himself died on a cross, apparently a failure, and yet by His death, He won us an eternal victory. For in that death, He atoned for the sins of mankind.

Jesus points out this paradox with the story of the apparently successful Pharisee and the sinful Publican both of whom went to the temple to pray (Luke 18:9-14). The Pharisee's prayer was boastful—unlike others, *he* had never let God down. By contrast, the Publican stood afar off and bowed his head in humility and prayed: "God be merciful to me a sinner." Commenting on this incident, Jesus said: "I tell you, this man [the Publican] went down to his house justified rather than the other [the Pharisee]." The man who appeared to be successful was a spiritual failure. The one who appeared to be a failure was the one who was indeed successful. Humility before God, not ability in the flesh, is the only true success.

When people fail, they usually do one of two things. Either they confess their failure, repent of it, and get right with God, or they go around making excuses for their failure. The first get back on track and ultimately turn their failure into success. The latter never honestly face their failure. They never solve the problems that led to it, and their lives never get turned around. God wants us not only to repent and erase our failures; He wants us to go on and find real success in serving Him.

The Failure Factor

Failure orientation is that self-perception found in some people that limits not only their self-confidence, but even their ability to trust in God as all-sufficient Sovereign. Individuals with a failure orientation are haunted by a sense of failure, which comes from one of two sources:

1. How we think we appear to others. If we are prone to a failure orientation, we tend to develop "ears" for negative feedback from others. Blocking out or downplaying positive feedback, the failure orientation makes us morbidly sensitive to any negative response we're getting from others. Unfortunately, we tend to limit the feedback we receive—thereby limiting whatever useful information we might glean from the comments of others. We need feedback from others to help us develop the foundation stones of our value system, self-concept, and understanding of behavior.

Individuals with a failure orientation have trouble distinguishing between negative feedback directed at them personally and negative feedback simply directed at their behavior. It is important to be able to distinguish between the two in interpreting feedback. "Failure" that may come in the form of a negative response to one's behavior is usually short-lived and may be overcome. Such "failure" should not be mistaken for a negative response to one's own person or self-integrity. As Christians, we may fail, but we are not failures. Whatever others choose to think of us, we are "more than conquerors through Jesus Christ who loves us" (*see* Romans 8:37). From time to time, others may praise us or ridicule us, but we must never lose our true identity and sense of purpose in the quicksand of struggling to prove ourselves acceptable to others. The Scriptures describe clearly how we should envision our efforts as we strive to achieve our goals in this life: "Whatever you do, do your work heartily, as for the Lord rather than for men; knowing that from the Lord you will receive the reward of the inheritance. It is the Lord Christ whom you serve" (Colossians 3:23, 24 NAS).

2. How we view ourselves. None of us can help measuring himself against his own expectations and standards. Frequently, a person with a failure orientation has an artificially high, unrealistic, or even perfectionistic set of expectations for himself. When asked to rate their accomplishments in almost any area on a scale from one to ten, such persons inevitably rate themselves at five or worse. They rate themselves harshly, even when by all objective standards their performance is far above average. These individuals tend to generalize or categorically classify themselves as total successes or total failures. They have an "either-or" mentality when viewing their own accomplishments. They see their output as fully acceptable or totally worthless—more often the latter. Such a sense of failure often paralyzes initiative. The person becomes cautious, diffident, unwilling to take risks his own judgment tells him are perfectly acceptable. Such persons need a comparison group of other individuals who are at a roughly equivalent skill and attribute level with whom they can identify and derive a sense of belonging without either being intimidated or bored.

Overcoming the Failure Factor

1. Fully analyze and understand your own failure-prone thinking. Analyzing the negative thinking and feelings of failure within us can help in identifying the various areas or aspects of life in which they appear. Try to delineate these areas as specifically as possible and look for hidden irrational ideas or unbiblical beliefs that serve to undermine your sense of God-given worth. Usually you can trace your failure orientation back to various setbacks and misconceptions coming from ideas about yourself, your friends, job, parents, brothers and sisters, church, or school. Stop perceiving the world through your mind's outdated "failure filter," but rather begin to analyze and approach situations from a biblical basis. On a piece of paper, write down every irrational or unbiblical idea you find. Then match it with a passage of Scripture that refutes it.

2. Choose goals and objectives that will improve your self-concept. It is advisable to begin with an area in which you have a reasonable amount of self-confidence. A success-oriented self-concept is contagious within our own personality. When we are able to establish goals and begin to reach them, the belief that "I can do all things through Christ Jesus who strengthens me" begins to take on genuine reality in our own experience. From one area of success, this attitude of confident capability will snowball into other personal and professional areas in our life.

3. Break the objectives down into "bite size" components. Once we have begun to take on an objective, it is necessary to approach that goal through a series of small steps. No one can jump up onto the roof of a house, but ten or twelve small steps on a ladder will get us there just the same. By breaking the goal down into a series of smaller, "bite size" behaviors and objectives, we simplify our task and heighten our chances for success. These smaller objectives should be undertaken in logical sequence, moving from shortest to longest or easiest to hardest. Here, the wise and thoughtful counsel of a spiritually mature person is invaluable, whether we need advice or just encouragement.

4. Implement a plan of action. This is the trial-and-error step. It will involve developing persistence above all else. It will involve the discipline to be well prepared for a task, and sensitivity to remain teachable and flexible. A change in a personal failure orientation of a longstanding nature won't happen overnight. Many times, in fact, we will find ourselves taking two steps forward and one back, but time is on our side, and the outcome is guaranteed, "For I am confident of this very thing, that He who began a good work in you will perfect it until the day of Christ Jesus" (Philippians 1:6 NAS).

Turn Your Failure Into Success

Many people never overcome their failures because they never really forgive themselves for failing. They continue to punish themselves with self-inflicted guilt, rather than moving beyond failure to success.

1. To fail is to be human. All human beings fail. God is fully aware of your limitations. "For He knows our frame; He remembers that we are dust" (Psalms 103:14 NKJV). "For all have sinned, and come short of the glory of God" (Romans 3:23). True success is not avoiding failure, but learning what to do with it.

2. To fail is not to be a failure. Studies show that the most successful people often fail. For example, Babe Ruth not only set the record in his day for home runs in a single baseball season—he led the league in strikeouts, as well. No one would call Babe Ruth a failure, but many Christians are quick to call themselves failures when they suffer a few strikeouts in life.

3. No one is ever a failure until he stops trying. It is better to attempt much and occasionally fail, than to attempt nothing and achieve it. No one learns the limits of his ability until he has reached the point of total failure. Thomas Edison tried over five thousand different types of light-bulb filaments without success before finding one that would work. His willingness to endure many failures without branding himself a failure gave us the modern electric light.

4. Failure is never final as long as we get up one more time than we fall down. Fear is much more damaging than failure. If you've failed, admit it and start over. Forgive yourself and learn to forgive others. Don't be controlled by what has happened to you, but rather be controlled by where you are trying to go. Focus on your goals, not your failures. Move ahead with determination, for nothing worthwhile is accomplished without some risk. "God has not given us a spirit of fear, but of power and of love and of a sound mind" (2 Timothy 1:7 NKJV). God has given you certain gifts and abilities to serve Him. You may also have certain limitations. You may not be able to do everything, but you can do something. Go and do it to His glory!

9

Fatigue

Ekluomai, to faint or become physically exhausted. Signifies a running down in energy and strength.

In an age of so much leisure, it is remarkable that so many thousands of Americans are chronically tired. Unfortunately, a great many of these tired Americans are Christians. All the possible causes of excessive fatigue or exhaustion are too numerous to mention here, but ask yourself if any of the following statements apply to you:

• "I am so wiped out at the end of the day that it's all I can do to undress and collapse into bed."

• "I feel more exhausted in the morning when I wake up than when I went to bed the night before."

• "I feel so drained of energy lately that I am barely able to get the necessities done at home or at the office."

If any of the above applies to you, examine the following four causes of fatigue.

1. Physical causes of fatigue. Physical overexertion can be a cause of chronic fatigue. However, in twentieth century America, this is very rare. By far the most common physical cause of fatigue in this country is underexertion. Our bodies were designed by God to take in food for energy, metabolize that food through strenuous physical effort, excrete the wastes, and rest appropriately. All this was intended to produce a healthy bodily "temple" in which the spirit of man and the Spirit of God could co-dwell. As man's technological ingenuity has increased, however, so has his ability to avoid exertion, and, thus, our physical bodies are often underused. Imagine buying a powerful sports car and never driving it more than five miles an hour, creeping back and forth to work and on errands. Eventually it would begin to sputter, misfire, and have trouble getting started. Such is the physical condition of many people. Regular and strenuous exercise—under the supervision of your family physician—is the key to overcoming the most common physical cause of fatigue—underexertion.

2. Pathological causes for fatigue. Pathological causes for fatigue are those that result from any physical illness or disorder. It is quite common after a major illness or surgical procedure to feel fatigued or burned out for several weeks. While recuperating, you should pace yourself and not rush back into full activity too soon. Otherwise you will only prolong your period of recovery. You may even suffer a relapse. Extended fatigue over several weeks, with no apparent physical cause and no real relief should be cause for concern and requires a thorough medical checkup. Chronic fatigue associated with any of the following symptoms should be investigated by your doctor as soon as possible.

These are widely known as cancer's seven warning signals:

- Change in bowel or bladder habits
- A sore that does not heal
- Unusual bleeding or discharge
- Thickening or lump in breast or elsewhere
- Indigestion or difficulty in swallowing
- Obvious change in wart or mole
- Nagging cough or hoarseness

3. Psychological causes for fatigue. General practitioners readily admit that nearly 50 percent of people coming to their offices with "physical" complaints really suffer from emotional disorders. Emotional problems, especially depression, anxiety, and worry, are by far the most common causes of extended fatigue. The body's fatigue-resistance system can, in time, be worn down by continual emotional and personal stress. The body has a tremendous ability to adjust to different situations and different pressures, but prolonged emotional unrest, generated by either internal psychological conflict or external situational stress, can lead to anatomical and physical changes in the body which produce fatigue, exhaustion, and often disease. Modern medical science is only beginning to understand the real and important link connecting our emotional state and our physical well-being.

4. Spiritual causes of fatigue. The Bible clearly teaches that man's spiritual and physical well-being are closely connected. Guilt—impenitent, continual sin—often lies at the root of bodily sickness or fatigue. In Psalms 32:3, we read, "When I was silent about my sin, my body began to waste away, and I found myself groaning all the day long" (author's paraphrase). The anxiety produced by continual or unconfessed sin can wear us down, leaving us tired and dispirited as we try to go about the business of living.

Five Cures for Fatigue

1. Maintain a clear conscience. The Scripture teaches that when a believer is involved in continual and unrepentant sin, even his prayers are ineffective before the Lord. Our anguish and isolation will, in turn, foster unremitting anxiety—an anxiety only cured by confession and the restoration of a right relationship with God. David, in the Old Testament, understood the necessary healing power of such a relationship: "I acknowledged my sin unto thee, and mine iniquity have I not hid. I said, I will confess my transgressions unto the Lord, and thou forgavest the iniquity of my sin" (Psalms 32:5).

2. Eat a well-balanced diet. A well-balanced diet depends on both the quantity and the quality of the food we eat. Three meals a day are best, at regular intervals. Early in the morning, eat something low in sugar but high in protein. Small amounts of caffeine, a cup of coffee, for instance, are acceptable, but you should never perk yourself up with coffee or sweets while omitting regular, well-balanced meals. Quick "pick-me-up" foods, wolfed down at odd hours, and occasional binge meals throughout the week, generally put on extra pounds. These, of course, are an added burden to the cardiovascular, respiratory, muscular, and skeletal systems of the human body, and they produce fatigue, too. The weight charts on page 82 should help you determine whether you're carrying extra weight that may be contributing to a sense of fatigue.

Not only is it important *how much* we eat; we should pay attention to *what* we eat. Americans usually have no trouble eating enough—or more than enough—protein.

Men Aged Twenty-five and Over

Height	Small Frame	Medium Frame	Large Frame
5'1"	109–117	115–126	123–138
5'2"	112–120	118–130	126–141
5'3"	115–123	121–133	129–145
5'4"	118–126	124–136	132–149
5'5"	120–130	127–140	135–153
5'6"	125–134	131–144	139–158
5'7"	129–138	135–149	144–163
5'8"	133–142	139–153	148–167
5'9"	137–147	143–157	152–171
5'10"	141–151	147–162	156–176
5'11"	145–155	151–167	161–181
6'0"	149–159	155–172	165–186
6'1"	153–164	159–177	170–191
6'2"	157–168	164–182	175–196
6'3"	161–172	169–187	179–201

Women Aged Twenty-five and Over

Height	Small Frame	Medium Frame	Large Frame
4'8"	90–96	94–105	102–117
4'9"	92–99	96–108	104–120
4'10"	94–102	99–111	107–123
4'11"	97–105	102–114	110–126
5'0"	100–108	105–117	113–129
5'1"	103–111	108–120	116–132
5'2"	106–114	111–124	119–136
5'3"	109–117	114–128	123–140
5'4"	112–121	118–133	127–144
5'5"	116–125	122–137	131–148
5'6"	120–129	126–141	135–154
5'7"	124–133	130–145	139–156
5'8"	128–138	134–149	143–161
5'9"	132–142	138–153	147–166
5'10"	136–146	142–157	151–171

Individuals between the ages of eighteen and twenty-five years should subtract one pound for each year under twenty-five years of age to arrive at their projected ideal weight.

However, there are seven essential vitamin groups our bodies can run low on, contributing to a sense of physical fatigue and loss of stamina.

• *Vitamin A.* Vitamin A is easily depleted by stress; it is necessary both for healthy skin and clear night vision. Foods which contain plenty of Vitamin A are liver, apricots, carrots, yellow squash, egg yolk, butter, and cream.
• *Vitamin B complex.* The B vitamins are the body's

"energy transfer" vitamins. They allow the body to utilize the calories it takes in for proper maintenance of function and growth. The vitamin B complex is also essential to the proper function and growth of the nervous system, and significant shortage of any of the vitamin B complex can lead not only to fatigue but to emotional symptoms consistent with depression. The B complex vitamins are widely available in wheat germ, eggs, pork, brewer's yeast, nuts, potatoes, legumes, and liver.

• *Vitamin C.*   Vitamin C has been recognized as essential in the body's defense against infections. There is also some evidence that Vitamin C, especially when taken in fresh fruits, may help retard hardening of the arteries—a condition usually caused by the buildup of cholesterol in the small blood vessels. Potatoes, cabbage, green peppers, tomatoes, and virtually all fruits are high in Vitamin C.

• *Vitamin D.*   Vitamin D is essential to the proper absorption and utilization of both phosphorus and calcium. For this reason, it is often added to the milk we buy commercially. Calcium and phosphorus are necessary for the repair and strengthening of bones. Butter, egg yolk, liver, and cod-liver oil are rich sources of Vitamin D.

• *Vitamin E.*   Vitamin E has been connected to the proper healing of wounds and may offer some protection against heart disease. Foods such as margarine, legumes, egg yolk, vegetable oil, and wheat germ are rich in vitamin E.

• *Vitamin K.*   Vitamin K is especially necessary for the proper health of the blood. Its main function is to insure that the blood clots properly and can, therefore, circulate through our bodies without hemorrhaging. (Should we sustain cuts or bruises, it is essential that the blood clot properly.) Vitamin K is richly available in leafy vegetables, vegetable oil, and pork liver.

3. Get regular exercise.   Not only does regular exercise help you do physical labor without getting tired, it actually helps you think better. You will need to choose the best time of day for exercising—that time varies from person to person. For some people, an early morning regimen is the best—one that leaves them braced and ready to meet the day. Others, if they can, exercise during the middle of the day, preferring a noon workout to the lavish executive lunch. Probably the most popular time is the late afternoon and early evening. People use that time to unwind both mentally and physically after a hard day's work on the job or at home. Ask your doctor how much exercise, and what kind, would be best for you. Any regular fitness program should produce the following:

• Better cardiovascular function (stronger heart and increased blood circulation).
• Lower blood pressure.
• Reduced levels of cholesterol and fats in the blood.
• Increased muscle size and strength. This will also increase bone strength over time and check your bones' tendency to lose calcium with advancing age.
• Reduction of excessive body fat.
• Increased physical stamina. You will be able to work longer at peak capacity, even speeding up under pressure.
• Recent experimental data suggest that being physically fit helps you both to concentrate better and remember better. This jibes with what many joggers say: The time they spend running "really clears my head and helps me concentrate when I get back to work."

4. Pace yourself. Save the hardest jobs for your peak times. Some people work best in the late afternoon. Others claim to be night people and do their best work in the late evening. Still others, who are morning people, are at their best during the first few hours of the day. To some extent, of course, the laws of the marketplace dictate when we may or may not tackle certain jobs.

5. Vacations, breaks, and sleep. All three are different ways both mind and body can rest and recuperate. You should take vacations when you most need them. In America, unfortunately, they are often more hectic and rigorously planned than regular jobs. Regular breaks taken throughout the day—a brisk walk or a friendly chat with a colleague—will often reduce fatigue and make you more productive. Proper sleep is crucial in avoiding fatigue and depends, in turn, on how fit you are, both physically and emotionally. Don't turn to narcotics like alcohol or sleeping pills, which only become less effective after time. God's original plan—work six days and rest one—still works. If you live right, work right, eat right, and sleep right, you will feel right. Exercise, watch your diet, and you will start to feel better immediately.

Finances

Mammonas, *name of a Syrian deity; hence,* **wealth.** *Synonymous with* **argurion,** *money.*

No one, according to Christ, can serve both God and mammon (Matthew 6:24; Luke 16:13), yet He also commanded His disciples to make "friends of the mammon of unrighteousness" (Luke 16:9). Scriptural teaching on money, we see, is balanced.

The key to Jesus' warning about mammon is found in the word *serve* (*douleuo*)—as in service rendered by a slave. His point is clear in the original Greek: One cannot be God's slave and, at the same time, the slave of money.

Money is *not* the root of all evil; the *love of money* is

the root of all evil (1 Timothy 6:10). Man's unbounded acquisitiveness often proves his undoing. Millions are corrupted by the desire for things. Yet, more believers attribute their financial decisions to "God's leading" than any other matter. When the bottom falls out, they are shocked, bitter, disillusioned. "How could God let this happen to me?"

A Christian View of Wealth

Being a Christian does not exempt one from God's laws governing finances. The Bible clearly teaches that money is God's gift entrusted to faithful stewards (Psalms 8:6; Luke 16:11; 2 Corinthians 8:15). This entails unswerving integrity in every area of our personal and business lives. True financial principles are never at odds with true spiritual ones. Christian ethics hold us strictly accountable for what we do with our money. Our individual plans and commitments cannot contradict our uniqueness as Christians. We are *in* the world, but we are not *of* the world (John 17:14–16). Money is simply a tool in spreading the Gospel (Luke 16:9–13). As such, though, it is temporary—a thing of this world. Things pass away. Only God, His Word, and His children remain forever.

For the Christian, wealth can be used in God's service. With it, we can build hospitals, churches, feed the poor, spread the Gospel, and so forth. Then, too, it can be wasted on self-indulgent living, frivolous activities, and sinful habits. The Bible warns that those who pursue money as an end in itself always die frustrated and unhappy. Such people never understand *why* they have money. When wealth is not used to God's glory, it corrupts its owner.

God has entrusted this world and its resources to mankind. Psalms 8:6 declares of man, "Thou dost make him to rule over the works of Thy hands" (NAS). The

Bible affirms God's blessing of wealth on men like Abraham, Job, and Solomon. The New Testament speaks of
wealthy Christians in the early Church, such as Joseph
of Arimathaea. At the same time, the Apostle Paul observed the early Christians were "not many wise ...
mighty [wealthy] ... [or] noble" (1 Corinthians 1:26).
The Bible condemns neither rich nor poor.

Private Property and Free Enterprise

The Scriptures often speak positively about buying
and selling, the legitimacy of the marketplace, and the
right of free individuals to own property. The very land
of Israel was God's gift to His people (Joshua 13:7;
21:43). The laws of economics are based upon the
Judeo-Christian principles of Scripture. In all Jesus'
parables about land owners (Matthew 20:1-16), He
never spoke against the concept of private enterprise.
What Jesus condemned was the misuse of wealth.

Wealth is seen as God's blessing (Proverbs 10:22), but
the oppression of the poor by the wealthy is clearly condemned (Proverbs 22:22, 23). At the same time, Scripture teaches that poverty does not necessarily reflect
God's judgment: "Better is the poor that walketh in his
integrity," declares Proverbs 19:1. The idea here is obvious—it is better to be poor, honest, and happy than to
be rich, guilty, and miserable. The Law commands fair
treatment for all men: "Ye shall do no unrighteousness
in judgment: thou shalt not respect the person of the
poor, nor honour the person of the mighty; but in righteousness shalt thou judge thy neighbour" (Leviticus
19:15, 16).

Happiness and Money

Money, we are often told, cannot buy happiness. Yet
millions expend their lives in the hope that it will. Their
lives become an unending quest for the unattainable.

Prosperity does not automatically produce happiness. Wealth itself is only temporary (Psalms 49:10-12). As we learn from Job, fortunes vanish overnight.

The real problem with trying to buy happiness is that it's just not for sale! God never made us to be satisfied with material things. Only by living above the material can we ever learn to use it properly. God's aim in giving is not hoarding, but sharing.

The Grace of Giving

The Bible admonishes us to develop the grace of giving (2 Corinthians 8:1-7). The churches of Macedonia are cited by the Apostle Paul as an example of joyful giving out of deep poverty. It is not getting that brings happiness, but giving. The apostle also notes that they first gave themselves to the Lord and then gave of their wealth. The totally committed Christian is one who knows the joy of giving. He is truly a cheerful giver (2 Corinthians 9:7).

Many believers are in financial trouble because they have never learned to give. They are obsessed with getting. They have missed the whole purpose of stewardship and discipleship in the area of finances. They love to talk of wealth and success as blessings from God, but they know little of the grace of giving. They want more as added proof of His favor. They never think of themselves as conduits of His grace to others.

Distorted Values

Our attitude toward money and possessions reflects our values. If you value yourself on the basis of what you have, you will be driven by the desire to succeed. If you think money alone will make you happy, you will never be happy. Joy is a fruit of the Spirit and a gift of God (Galatians 5:22). It is not for sale! The poorest believer may own it in abundance. It is not dependent upon our circumstances, because it comes from God. Only when we develop the right value system will we ever understand the proper place of money in our lives.

1. Money and wealth are temporary. That which is material is temporal. It will not last forever, and may not even last a lifetime. Only the spiritual is eternal. Therefore, spiritual priorities should always come before material priorities.

2. Christian stewardship is necessary. Temporary though it may be, we are commanded to be good stewards of what we possess (Matthew 25:14–30; Luke 12:16–21). Our money should be managed wisely, invested carefully, spent cautiously, and shared joyfully.

3. Wealth is to be used to God's glory. When we learn to use our possessions to promote the Gospel and invest in God's work, we begin to understand that God does not give us things as an end in themselves. They are to be used to honor Him (Proverbs 3:9).

Causes of Financial Problems

Financial problems can be traced back to a variety of causes:

1. Greed. The desire for more always leaves us dissatisfied with what we have. It tempts us to make unwise or extravagant purchases.

2. Pride. Sometimes we are driven by pride to want things we cannot afford because they make us look successful. They build up our image.

3. Ignorance. Many people simply cannot manage their money.

4. Laziness. Some people are broke because they will not work. Their financial problems are but symptoms of a deeper weakness.

5. Stinginess. The Bible clearly teaches that those who don't give, don't receive (Luke 6:38).

Financial Bondage

Financial bondage comes when people spend more than they make. It leaves them in bondage to their creditors, forever short of ready cash. The symptoms include:

- Overdue bills
- Financial worries
- Confusion
- Covetousness
- Financial manipulation
- Deceitfulness
- "Get-rich-quick" syndrome

Money brings you not blessing, but frustration. Financial conflicts are among the major causes of divorce. Women especially can worry about money; they fret when the bills are not paid, taking out their fears and frustrations on their husbands. Decisions are made hastily, and things go from bad to worse. Financial bondage usually leads to carelessness, impulse buying, speculation, and—worst of all—credit buying. Those who charge the most can usually afford the least, and their debts mount up. Getting out of debt becomes their overriding concern. They have little or no time to develop creative options toward financial growth.

Financial Freedom

In order to break free from financial bondage, several things are necessary.

1. Transfer "ownership" of all your possessions to God. Take your hands off. Recognize God's sovereign Lordship over you, your house, your car—everything. Acknowledge that everything you have, you have in trust.

2. Start tithing. As Christians under grace, we should view the Law's demand (10 percent) as a bare minimum. True Christian giving should be spontaneous and abundant. Tightwads get little from God (*see* 2 Corinthians 9:6–8).

3. *Write a budget.* You will never avoid nonessential purchases until you determine just what you must have in order to pay your bills (house, car, food, heat, lights, phone, and so forth).

4. *Stop all unnecessary purchases.* Stop buying things you cannot afford. Such buying is only plunging you deeper into debt and will jeopardize everything you have. Until you have things under control, eliminate unnecessary expenditures (new clothes, dinners out, expensive habits).

5. *Buy nothing on credit.* Pay cash for everything. Credit cards are convenient, but they plunge undisciplined buyers into ruin. "Get it today," we are told. "Pay for it tomorrow." Too often "tomorrow" becomes *indefinitely.*

6. *Sell fast-depreciating items.* If you are really in over your head, that Porsche may have to go. Four more years of high payments means you will owe more on it than it's worth. The same holds true for new furniture.

7. *Develop biblical priorities.* Spend your money on things that produce the greatest long-lasting benefit (like your children's education). Avoid temporary fads that are keeping you broke. Evaluate every purchase from God's perspective. Ask yourself: "How will buying this item help the cause of Christ?"

8. *Establish a working income.* You mustn't spend everything you make. Make allowances for tithing, taxes, fixed expenses, debt-retirement, savings, and so forth. Only about 70 percent of your total income should really go for actual living expenses.

9. *Learn money management.* In the Parable of the Talents (Matthew 25:14–29), Jesus condemns the poor money manager. Set proper priorities and learn to plan ahead.

10. Get out of debt.   It may be a wise decision to contact a capable accountant or investment counselor for some professional help and advice in setting up a workable plan for handling your finances. This can be done confidentially, it is usually relatively inexpensive, and it can really improve the effectiveness of your money management. You will never be financially free until you pay off your debts. Remember, your testimony is at stake. God's glory requires you do no less!

11

Frustration

Atheteo, *to deny someone a request, to say no. Thus, to cause frustration or futility.*

The Bible warns us that a "double minded" man is unstable in all his ways (James 1:8). Frustration always comes of trying to do too much at once. It also comes when we feel thwarted. Anyone who has ever been caught in a major traffic jam knows all about frustration!

The opposite of frustration is direction. When our way ahead is clear, we experience little or no frustration. Frustration comes when we keep running into obstacles. More than anything else, the frustrated person needs to control his feelings and find direction for life.

Don't Become a Victim of Your Feelings

Feelings are a normal part of everyday life. At a football game, we get excited; at a funeral, we are usually sad; at the grocery store, we often get frustrated; at a family reunion, we are filled with joy. Feelings affect, and often control, the greater part of our lives. They represent our perception of our physical and emotional condition. Thus, we often say, "I *feel* great!" or, "I *feel* lousy." We even stretch the word *feeling* to include attitudes, judgments, and convictions. "How do you feel about our foreign policy?" someone asks. The answer is not a statement of one's feelings, but one's beliefs.

We live in a feeling-oriented society. "If it feels good, do it!" is the existential motto of our age. Everyone seems to be giving in to their feelings and setting aside their convictions. Traditional beliefs yield to the narcissistic pursuit of self-gratification. Feelings are everything—a principle that has betrayed many a Christian into outright sin. Excuses are legion: "But I feel so much better when I'm with her." "Can't I do this and still love God?" "Doesn't God want us to be happy?" What we are really questioning is often God's revealed Word.

Feelings Are Symptoms

Our emotions tells us what is really going on inside us. They are often by-products of our thinking. If, for example, we think a human being dies at death, then the death of a loved one will leave us prostrate. If we think that we are ugly or inferior, we will *feel* ugly or inferior. Inferiority in itself is not a feeling; it is a value judgment we make about ourselves. Guilt, likewise, is a feeling—one that comes from behavior. If you do something you think wrong, you will feel guilty.

Some people do not *feel* saved. That should not surprise us, since the conviction that one is saved is not an emotion. Assurance is not a feeling, but a belief. Distinguishing between our feelings and our beliefs and behavior is essential to solving our problems. Our attitudes reflect our true inner beliefs about ourselves and our problems. "I can't" really means "I won't!" Anxiety, hatred, envy, grief, fear—all reflect how we think. Nonbiblical thinking will always result in nonbiblical actions. For example, nonbiblical thinking tells you that you have a right to do whatever you want, and if someone tries to stop you, you will retaliate. Biblical revelation, however, tells you not to strike back (1 Timothy 3:3) and to turn the other cheek (Matthew 5:39).

Feelings Can Be Dangerous

Our feelings are but symptoms of our true inner thinking. They are changeable when our thoughts and beliefs change. Feelings are guides to help us better understand what's occuring within our personality. They are not good guides for establishing a permanent course of action. To encourage people to impulsively follow their feelings rather than God's Word is the worst advice any Christian could ever give another. To deny your feelings and resolve to do what is right is not hypocrisy, but character. Consider—at least once every day of your life, you defy every feeling in your body: You get out of bed!

Irresponsible people are perennial victims of their own feelings. You may feel like skipping school, robbing a bank, shooting your neighbor, or running away. That does not mean that any of those feelings are the right thing to do. Christian morality (behavior) is clearly outlined in the Word of God. The Bible itself is the final authority for our lives—not our feelings.

Deny Your Feelings

Self-discipline comes only when we learn the art of self-denial. We are in a lifelong struggle against our feelings. In order to live the Spirit-controlled life, we must die to ourselves. The Scripture admonishes: ". . . present your bodies a living sacrifice, holy, acceptable unto God . . . And be not conformed to this world: but be ye transformed by the renewing of your mind . . ." (Romans 12:1, 2). We have to learn to think like Christians in order to behave like Christians. We need to think biblically in order to behave biblically. Right thinking and right behavior will then result in right feelings. You will feel right when you know you have done right.

Emotional people let their feelings rule every aspect of their lives. While we need to understand how we really feel and why we feel that way, we can never let our feelings become the final standard of right and wrong. One woman may feel good about her abortion, while another feels guilty. A husband may feel his divorce is of God, while his wife feels that it is of the devil! Who is right? Are all feelings relative to each person's own experience and perception? If they are, then the statements and commands of Scripture are meaningless and can be quickly dismissed by those who feel they do not apply to them.

The ultimate standard by which we must judge our feelings is the Word of God. No matter how I feel, God's Word gives me an unbiased declaration of His truth. Remember, Jesus said, "You shall know the truth, and the truth shall make you free" (John 8:32 NAS). God's truth liberates us from our feelings. Truth sets the soul free for fellowship with God. It is His Word of truth that sanctifies the believer and equips him for life and service. No matter how you feel, one truth stands paramount above all others—God loves you!

Dealing With Life's Frustrations

Frustration is a part of life. Nobody ever went through life without experiencing some frustration. Problems come into our lives which try our faith and sometimes even push us to our very limits. But in every problem, no matter how frustrating, God is at work in your life. Scripture tells us to "let the peace of God rule in your hearts" (Colossians 3:15). Others may be upset, disturbed, erratic, emotional, violent, or bitter. You can remain calm in the midst of the storm, because God is in control.

Peace does not come naturally. The Scripture tells us to let the peace of God rule in our hearts. We must allow His peace to conquer our deepest frustrations. How? "Let the word of Christ dwell in you richly in all wisdom . . ." (Colossians 3:16). One can only allow the Word of God to control his life when he is reading it and living it. The implication is that the Word of Christ does not automatically dwell within us. We must read, meditate upon it, memorize it. The Scripture does not automatically dwell in your heart. You must put it there.

When problems come into our lives, we tend to react emotionally, without ever considering that we may be reacting in a totally non-Christian manner. By so doing we fail to let the truth of God's Word capture our souls. Therefore, we are not living under the control of the Holy Spirit. The result is invariably an explosion of emotional frustration.

Finding Direction

The will of God is revealed in the Word of God. The two are never contradictory. God will never lead you to do something contrary to His revealed Word. Nor will His Word ever contradict His will for your life. God has a wonderful plan for your life, but you will only find it by submission to His will.

Frustration always comes of doubting or denying God's will. If you have gotten off the track, get back on again. You will never find peace outside God's revealed will for your life. If you find yourself stalled in one of life's lanes, then learn to accept your "life-jam" as a divine halt on the road of life. Stop trying to run, if God wants you to sit and listen. In time, the master traffic director will have you going again when you are ready to navigate properly.

Life's frustrations are but divinely appointed delays. They are time-outs giving God a chance to work. Don't give up the race. The last lap has yet to be run!

12

Guilt

Hupodikos, *brought to trial, liable to be tried.* *Liable for doing something wrong.*

Guilt comes from a troubled conscience. It is a self-judgment based on perceived personal misconduct. It may or may not deepen into sorrow or remorse. Some people, in fact, sublimate their guilt. The Bible tells us (1 Timothy 4:2) their consciences are seared, and they seldom show regret for what they do.

Sin Is a Major Cause of Guilt

All sin initially produces guilt in the soul of the sinner. When guilt weighs heavy on the sinful soul, it drives us to God for forgiveness. If, however, we fail to obtain that forgiveness, or if we persist in our sin, we may deaden (sear) our consciences and become no longer sensitive to guilt. Nevertheless, we are still guilty before God. A murderer may feel no remorse for his crime but pay the penalty just the same. Whether we sin ignorantly or willfully, we stand condemned before the law (Romans 2:12).

The Psychological Effects of Guilt

Guilt is a major factor in psychological problems. No one is a stranger to guilt.

Often we respond to it with defense mechanisms—denial, blame shifting, suppression, sublimation, self-justification, and so forth. All these, in fact, are means that the personality uses instinctively to deal with guilt on a psychological level. Guilt feelings stimulate self-condemnation in the form of anxiety, inferiority, fear, worry, and pessimism. When these are not resolved, they lead to psychological camouflage, to diversionary behaviors such as drug abuse or sexual acting out, and eventually to depression.

So-called "False Guilt"

All guilt is real guilt. A person is guilty, by biblical definition, when he has broken God's moral law (Romans 3:19). Also by biblical definition, a person's sins (and his real guilt) are washed away when confession occurs (1 John 1:9). However, guilt feelings are another matter. A person may be guilty of sin and yet not feel guilty. Another person may feel guilty over something that is not sinful, due to his false standard of righteousness. Guilt feelings based on a personal sense of chronic inferiority before God are referred to as "false guilt." These guilt feelings are real enough, but it is the standard by which we judge ourselves as inferior that is false. The standard may indeed not be legitimate (dreams of unattainable perfection, for instance), but our willful violation of that standard will still produce a real sense of guilt. The solution to false guilt is to acknowledge and correct our false standards, not merely explain away our guilty feelings.

For example, a person may grow up being told that it is sinful to wear red socks. Because he believes that standard to be true, but chooses to violate it, he will experience guilt. The solution is not to deny the reality of that guilt, but to force the individual to reexamine his standard. Once he or she is convinced the standard is invalid, the guilt will disappear.

The Moral Conflict

It is precisely in the area of dealing with guilt that Christian theology and secular psychology have their greatest conflict. If there is no God and, therefore, no divine standard of behavior, there is no true guilt. All guilt would then be false guilt arising from a faulty value system. Guilt would merely be the result of violating generally accepted cultural mores, rather than universal principles. In a culture where murder, cannibalism, rape, adultery, incest, or stealing was acceptable behavior, there would be no real guilt for those acts.

Christianity will have none of this! We believe that real guilt arises from sinful actions that can only be truly forgiven by God.

Objective Guilt

Objective guilt is personal guilt resulting from the violation of an objective standard: legal, social, personal, or divine. Violating civil law, social law, or our own personal standards results in real guilt, as does the violation of God's laws. In order to face the issue of objective guilt, we must acknowledge the legitimacy of the standard that condemns us. Correction and restoration are possi-

ble because we recognize an objective standard of behavior.

Subjective Guilt

Subjective guilt is the sense of regret, shame, or condemnation we experience when we believe we have done
wrong. Such feelings are not always bad, as they may be
the result of sinful behavior. These guilt feelings may
cause us to face our sin and deal with it. However, some
may feel guilty out of proportion to their act of sin. Subjective guilt is a fallible and sometimes irrational judgment we pass on ourselves. It is self-condemnation
generating feelings of worthlessness. Subjective guilt
varies with our feelings about ourselves and the way we
act. It is based on a fallible measure, rather than an objective standard.

Resolving Guilt by Repentance and Confession

Two principles stand clear in Scripture for resolving
guilt: repentance and confession. Repentance (Greek,
metanoia) is a mental decision that produces an act of
the will. When we change our mind about our sin, we do
something about that sin. No one ever truly repented
and then went on sinning. Confession (Greek, *homolo-
geo*) means to "say the same thing" or to agree. When
we confess, we do not simply declare, "I have sinned."
We acknowledge that God's judgment on that sin is just.
The Bible promises: "If we confess our sins, he is faithful
and just to forgive us our sins, and to cleanse us from all
unrighteousness" (1 John 1:9).

The *means,* then, of dealing with guilt is repentance,
and the *method* is confession. The *goal* is the freedom of
one's conscience. True repentance and confession lead
to a clear conscience, which heals the guilty soul. Without a clear conscience, guilt cannot be resolved. Those

who refuse to repent of sin will persist in that sin. Those who refuse to confess their sin will pretend things are resolved when they are not. You will never be free from guilt until you face your sin and do something about it.

1. *Acknowledge any hidden personal sin that is the root of your guilt.* Pinpoint wrong attitudes and actions that are eating you up with guilt. Be totally honest with God. He already knows what you have done: "... for the Lord searches all hearts, and understands every intent of the thoughts . . ." (1 Chronicles 28:9 NAS). Prayerfully ask the Holy Spirit of God to illuminate those areas of your life that are not pleasing to God.

2. *Honestly face the sin that is feeding your guilt.* Choose a point at which to clean the slate with God and start over. Do not just admit you have failed. Establish a turning point in your life. Face your sin, confess it, correct it, and forget it. Discard any inferior, irrational, or unbiblical standard you've been comparing yourself to and beating yourself down with. These may be breeding painful false guilt feelings.

3. *Make a complete confession of your sin.* Come to terms with God about the seriousness of your sin. Stop making excuses, and take full responsibility for what you have done. Two marks of genuine confession are *sorrow* according to the will of God and *repentance* without remorse (Psalms 101:3; 119:145).

4. *Plan to avoid future failure.* See your sin as unwise and self-defeating. Proverbs 8:36 reminds us: "He who sins against me injures himself . . ." (NAS). Realize that tomorrow will be a better day if you conquer sin today. Live to glorify God, not to satisfy yourself. Correcting your problem will bring glory to Him and be an encouragement to others. Totally dedicate yourself to victory.

Accepting Forgiveness

Some sins we simply cannot forgive ourselves for. Yet the Bible assures us only one sin is really unpardonable—blasphemy against the Holy Spirit. All others may be forgiven! We must learn to take God's offer of forgiveness seriously. Jesus constantly emphasized that He came to save sinners, not condemn them (John 3:17). By condemning ourselves, we reject God's offer of grace and cleansing. We refuse the only true solution to our problem of guilt.

Salvation is instantaneous, but it initiates a lifelong process. Conversion happens in a split second, but spiritual growth takes a lifetime. Learning to face our failures and the guilt they produce is part of that process. No one is perfect; no human being is error free. We are all guilty before God, yet He who knows us best is willing to forgive and forget.

13

Insecurity

Hettaomai, *to be less, or inferior; the opposite of* **hikanos,** *enough, sufficient.*

Insecurity means being unsure of yourself and your circumstances. If you were standing on a frozen lake of ice and suddenly heard it crack, you would become very insecure! You might not know whether to run, panic, pray, or yell for help, but you would definitely feel insecure. Insecure people often find themselves running around in total panic and confusion.

Inferiority means that a person has judged himself to be inadequate. People become insecure because of a sense of inferiority. Measuring yourself by someone else's yardstick, you will almost always come up short.

You can always find someone bigger, stronger, smarter, or prettier than yourself.

Insecurity and Self-image

Self-image reflects the value we put on ourselves. A poor self-image (based on insecurity and a sense of inferiority) will affect our attitudes toward ourselves, family, friends, and God. Insecurity makes us do several things that only compound the problem:

- *Fear the will of God*
- *Resist authority*
- *Use wrong methods to gain acceptance*
- *Be preoccupied with the way we look*
- *Daydream about being someone else*

Using the Wrong Measuring Stick

The Apostle Paul warns us not to measure ourselves by ourselves (2 Corinthians 10:12). Either way, the results are always damaging, because we tend to have an inflated opinion of ourselves and measure with such a small yardstick or because we undervalue ourselves and measure against a standard we cannot reach. We will always find someone brighter or abler than ourselves. We then become bitter and blame God for slighting us. *He has doled out His gifts unfairly,* we think. *He cannot be trusted.* In effect, we spurn God's plan for our life.

The Bible clearly teaches that we are God's unique creation. Even our physical appearance is no accident; we were intended by God to be what we are. In Psalms 139:14, David exclaims: "I will praise thee; for I am fearfully and wonderfully made: marvellous are thy works; and that my soul knoweth right well." He was rejoicing in God's design for his life. He was not reproaching God for His workmanship. "My body works properly," he is saying, "because God *intended* it to work properly!"

Accepting God's Design

Each person is uniquely designed by God for a special purpose in life. That design was chosen in eternity past, and established at conception. Psalms 139:15, 16 says: "My substance was not hid from thee, when I was made in secret . . . Thine eyes did see my substance, yet being unperfect; and in thy book all my members were written, which in continuance were fashioned, when as yet there was none of them."

The word *substance* comes from the Hebrew term meaning "embryonic mass." This passage plainly states that God did not leave your conception to chance—He had His hand on you from the very beginning! Those tiny cells had everything they needed to make you what you are now. He chose which cells would unite in order to determine your physical characteristics. There were just two at first—but God used them and made them multiply. He had a full-grown person in mind. He had *you* in mind.

The very members of our body were fashioned (developed) from that original unperfect (undeveloped) substance (embryo). Your arms, legs, hands—yes, even your face—were designed by God from the genetic makeup of your parents. No mere chance made you male or female; it was God's doing. Accept yourself for what you are, and you accept God's will for your life. All the worry and fretting in the world cannot change the color of a single hair. If you can trust God to save you, then you can trust His plan for your life. David responded by exclaiming, "How precious also are thy thoughts unto me, O God! how great is the sum of them!" (Psalms 139:17.) He was overwhelmed by God's goodness!

Getting Down on Yourself

Few issues in the Christian faith are more misunderstood than "self-concept" or "self-image." The Scriptures teach on one hand that the Christian must have the capacity to love himself (Matthew 22:39), yet at the same time, they condemn pride or complacency (Galatians 6:3). The proper mean is a self-concept that recognizes clearly no human being is worthy before God apart from the death, burial, and resurrection of Jesus Christ. Christ's intercessory work on our behalf must be personally accepted, in order to receive salvation. Though we are but lumps of clay in God's hand, nevertheless, we can become valuable vessels of service to Him. No one is unusable when Christ is in his life.

Five "Down-casters"

"Down-casters" are the things in a Christian's life that undermine self-esteem and foster a negative self-concept. These five are the most damaging:

1. Discouraging comments. In Acts 19:9, we find Paul faced with a curious problem. He had come to Ephesus in Asia Minor, and God had blessed his preaching there with some new Christian converts. As was his wont, Paul had begun to reason and debate with local religious leaders, seeking both to win them to Christ and to bolster the faith of the new converts who were present. Certain community leaders, however, were also present—men quick to assail the claims of the Gospel. These could only undermine the faith of young Christians. Paul, therefore, withdrew them from Ephesus and taught them privately. He realized how vulnerable we often are to remarks made by others—especially people we have come to respect—people like teachers, church members, even other friends.

As Christians, God accepts us, loves us, and sees enormous potential in our lives. It is neither wise nor productive to spend time with people who only discourage us, both as human beings in our own right and human beings whom Christ can use. People like this, in a sense, corrupt the "good morals" of a sound walk with God and hence damage the believer's self-image. The Scripture warns us we should avoid them: "Be not deceived: evil communications corrupt good manners [morals]" (1 Corinthians 15:33).

2. Unfair comparisons. The Bible teaches that God gives us a sphere of influence in which we fulfill ourselves by doing His will (*see* 2 Corinthians 10:15 NAS). Unreal or unfair comparisons often make us hard on ourselves. Another person may need different intellectual, physical, or artistic skills to function where God has put him. Comparisons only produce one of the following: *pride* or *self-rejection*. With pride, we assume our "sphere of influence" is bigger and better. With self-rejection, we conclude our "sphere of influence" is poorer and humbler. Either is displeasing to our Lord, who wants us to work and bear fruit where He has put us, finding fulfillment in doing His will (*see* 2 Timothy 4).

3. Negative thinking. Many times, doubts about our own worth come from past experiences, when we got in the habit of slighting ourselves and our accomplishments. Such negative conditioning is either "taught" or "caught." In either case, negative thinking about oneself and one's abilities is disastrous. The Apostle Paul warned young Timothy to stay clear of it: "Let no man despise thy youth [look down on you]; but be thou an example of the believers, in word, in conversation, in charity, in spirit, in faith, in purity" (1 Timothy 4:12).

4. Academic difficulty. In this age of computers and rising young technocrats, the pressure to perform intellectually can be fierce. It is true that as Christians we are to work hard and do our best (*see* Colossians 3:23). Such pressure, however, can open up cracks in our self-image. It can do lasting damage to young people who excel in areas other than academics.

5. *Unreasonable expectations.* The Apostle Paul
was a man who drove himself to achieve God's best for
his life. He described himself as "pressing toward the
mark," for the prize of fulfilling God's goals for him. And
yet, Paul knew each man or woman must work out those
goals before the Lord. Lofty or unreasonable expectations only make us feel hampered, constricted by ideals.
Eventually they weaken and overthrow our own image.
In his letter to the Philippians, Paul not only gives us his
own goals, he urges us to wait upon God as we try to set
goals for ourselves. Here both the Scriptures and the
Holy Spirit are essential. We need to avoid unreasonable
expectations. We should adopt goals which both stretch
our horizons and remain within reach.

Five "Up-lifters"

Just as the five "Down-casters" always undermine a
positive self-concept, the following five "Up-lifters" do
the opposite. They help build self-esteem.

1. *Accept God's purpose.* The first step entails
faith that God has given us the potential for something
wonderful. Whatever failures we have undergone, however discouraged we may be about ourselves, we are still
created in God's image (*see* Genesis 1:26). As a young-
ster once said, "God don't make no junk!"

2. *Know and do God's will.* If you have never accepted Christ as your personal Lord and Savior, start by
doing so. Become a member of God's family (*see* John
1:12), then make God's Word your steady diet. The
Bible puts it this way: "As newborn babes, desire the
pure milk of the word, that you may grow thereby"
(1 Peter 2:2 NKJV). Going on with the Lord means becoming fruitful. Here only the Holy Spirit can help. Only
the Holy Spirit can produce these qualities, that fruit
God longs to see in your life. As you grow as a Christian,

you will see more and more traces of the Spirit's work—erasing negative impressions and deepening your awareness that you are now a sanctified vessel in God's hand.

3. *Involve yourself in the lives of other people.* Nothing cures self-pity and low self-esteem like a healthy concern for others! Throughout the New Testament, both Christ and His apostles are shown constantly giving themselves to other people. Difficulties or tribulations never stopped them. The very night before His crucifixion, Christ prayed for the needs of others. Even amid our troubles, we can do the same.

4. *Work hard and persevere.* In Philippians 4:13, Paul triumphantly declares, "I can do all things through Christ who strengthens me" (NKJV). He did not make the remark lightly. The Church had known persecution, and the young Christians there had undergone much hardship. Yet there are times when all we can do is hang on. At such times, there is no substitute for grit. We mustn't knuckle under to discouragement. True Christian maturity is the prize, if only we stay the course.

5. *Be patient.* In the last analysis, we believe God is patient with us. He puts up with our blunders, forgives our sins, and helps us to maturity in Christ. The truth is, He wants even more than we do to see us develop a sound self-concept. He wants us to be mature Christians for our own good and for His glory. We have His Word, however long the process, He will never forsake us. We sometimes tend to run ahead of God; slow down and wait for Him.

Security Comes From God

Security comes of accepting God's will in our lives. It is the untroubled knowledge that an all-wise God means nothing but good. His will is *perfect* in every way (*see* Romans 12:2). It is the certainty of God's love. The Scripture reminds us that, "God commendeth his love toward us, in that, while we were yet sinners, Christ died for us" (Romans 5:8). He loves you so much that He gave His Son to die for your sins. He invites you to trust Him as your personal Savior and become His child.

Security comes when we realize that God knows all about us and loves us anyway! We can learn to live above our failures, our inadequacies, our mistakes, and our circumstances because we personally know the God who is greater than our greatest fears. He loves us with a binding commitment that will not let us go. Thus, the apostle can ask: "Who shall separate us from the love of Christ? shall tribulation, or distress, or persecution, or famine, or nakedness, or peril, or sword?" (Romans 8:35.) He then answers his own question: "Nay, in all these things we are more than conquerors through him that loved us" (v. 37). God's love is a love that never gives way.

Our personal security does not come from within. The human spirit by itself can never produce it. Rather, it is founded on the indwelling Holy Spirit—the One that "beareth witness with our spirit, that we are the children of God" (Romans 8:16). He is the very life of God living within every born-again believer. We are sealed by Him to God the Father, and our life is "hid with Christ in God" (Colossians 3:3). We are secure spiritually and personally in the love of God; insecurity has no claim over our lives. We can face any circumstance of life in the secure confidence that God is there, that He is in control, and that He loves us!

Three Steps to Claiming God's Security in Your Life

1. Believe that God is good. The prophet Jeremiah captured the essence of God's unchanging love for His children when he recorded the following words: " 'For I know the plans that I have for you,' declares the

Lord, 'plans for welfare and not for calamity to give you a future and a hope' " (Jeremiah 29:11 NAS). Not only does God intend to see us through the roughest times of our lives, but He also intends to bless us in the process.

2. Accept the fact that we are fully responsible for our own behavior. Modern humanistic philosophy tends to deny this, putting the blame on heredity, upbringing, or whatnot. Nothing could be further from the truth. From Genesis to Revelation, Scripture holds man squarely responsible for what he does. No one can *make* us unhappy, angry, rebellious. No one can *make* us sin. Whatever life hands us, how we respond is our choice alone. We can choose to obey God or disobey.

3. Believe by faith that God will deliver you through any situation. There are sixty-six books in the Bible, and all confirm this promise. As believers, we must take it on faith. "The Lord is near to all who call upon Him, To all who call upon Him in truth. He will fulfill the desire of those who fear Him; He will also hear their cry and will save them" (Psalms 145:18, 19 NAS).

Faith is a willingness to trust God amid both the warm winds of prosperity and the gales of adversity. Faith is both a rock of stability and a key that opens the door to God's provision in our lives. "And without faith it is impossible to please Him, for he who comes to God must believe that He is, and that He is a rewarder of those who seek Him" (Hebrews 11:6 NAS).

14

Jealousy

Zēlos, zeal, jealousy. Often leads to strife.

Jealousy is an attitude of envy or resentment toward others. Jealous people are usually nervous and irritable. They are constantly at odds with other people. They downgrade others in order to enhance their own self-esteem. They are often suspicious, obstinate, and evil tongued. The jealous person resents those who seem to be more successful and wishes he had what they have.

The root of jealousy is self-pity: the assumption that our needs are being slighted now, and probably always will be. It turns an unfriendly eye on the blessings, possessions, and opportunities of others. Jealousy is the ultimate selfishness! It makes us focus on the externals of

life: money, position, prestige, security, success. It leads
to bitterness, hostility, and vengefulness.

Jealousy is self-seeking zeal gone out of control. Because of its selfish nature, it inevitably leads to personal
conflicts. The jealous person cannot bear to see people
succeed. He refuses to rejoice in the blessings of others.
The Scripture admonishes us to "rejoice with them that
do rejoice, and weep with them that weep" (Romans
12:15). The jealous person can do neither! Since he refuses to rejoice in other's blessings, he cannot sympa-
thize in their hurts.

Self-pity Is Self-destructive

Self-pity is the ultimate protest against God's provi-
dence. It is the refusal to be content with God's provision for your life. It is a selfishness that demands the
"right" to have more, be more, do more. Self-pity will ultimately lead to rebellion and despair. The psalmist
David admitted that when he became jealous of the
wicked, he nearly stumbled (Psalms 73:2, 3).

Self-pity is really an expression of our anger toward
God. It is the ultimate cause of depression and suicide. It
leads to senseless brooding over the circumstances of
life. It fixes our thoughts on the negatives of life and
denies the possibility of improvement or change. It finally produces such personal misery that we lose the joy
of living. It works like this:

Self-pity → Anger → Bitterness → Depression

When this chain of self-destruction remains unbroken,
it will lead to deep despair. *Self-pity is being angry that
I am not what I want to be.* As long as we keep demanding more out of life, we will never be satisfied with what
we have. Contentment is one of life's most precious ben-
efits, but the jealous person will never find it. True contentment comes only when we relinquish our rights,
instead of asserting them.

Envy: The Enemy Within

Jealousy is caused by envy (Greek, *phthonos,* "ill will"), which leads to covetousness. Envy is the quality of never being satisifed. It covets what others have in a selfish attempt to reinforce one's own inadequacies. It only seeks its own welfare; it is deaf and blind to the needs of others. Envy is a driving force of self-destruction. It, too, forms a chain of self-destruction:

Envy → Covetousness → Frustration → Hostility

Envy is anger that I do not have what I want. Envy can eat up your soul until you hate people without reason. The envious person will actually speak out or strike out against others. He thinks that life, and therefore God, have been unfair to him. He wants to get back at God by getting at those He has blessed.

Surrender Your Rights

You will never overcome jealousy until you develop true contentment. The only way to eliminate jealousy is to cut it off at its root of self-pity. Contentment only comes when we surrender our rights to God. As long as we keep insisting that we have a right to a better deal, we will never be content.

Self-pity comes of clinging to our rights. It enslaves us to the past, so we cannot develop our future potential. Jealousy and its two sisters, envy and bitterness, make life miserable. They are not solutions to our problems. They are self-centered hurts that keep us from finding real solutions.

Design a Plan of Action

1. Admit your selfishness. Identify self-pity for what it is—sin! Stop dwelling on your hurts and disappointments; self-pity will not ease your pain or heal your hurting heart. Nor will it give you comfort or contentment. It will only drive you to despair.

2. Deny yourself.   One of the clearest conditions of discipleship is learning to deny yourself, take up your cross daily, and follow Christ (Luke 9:23). Life is a battle with self. Insist upon victory over every selfish desire. Settle for nothing less.

3. Surrender your rights.   Stop demanding your rights. Surrender them to God and accept whatever He gives back to you as privileges. Jealousy is not caused by our circumstances but by how we respond to our circumstances. Stop *reacting* to your circumstances, and start *responding* to God's working in your life. He is no fool who gives up what he cannot keep to gain what he cannot lose.

4. Realize who you are in Christ.   As a child of God, you are a joint heir with Jesus Christ. You have nothing to be jealous of. Why should you envy someone else, when you have God living within you? Yours is the heritage of eternal life. Heaven is your destiny! Jealousy is a waste of your time and energy. In Him we are overcomers. We all have one thing in common: We have overcome obstacles to get where we are now. Stop feeling sorry for yourself. You are a child of the King—live like it!

5. Start helping others.   The best way to forget your own troubles is to help someone else with his. Accept the responsibility of being a blessing to someone else. Stop waiting for others to bless you. Start being a blessing and you will receive a blessing. Develop a positive attitude that realizes your struggles can help you meet the needs of others. Learn to bear someone else's burden (Galatians 6:2) and yours will become lighter. God will give you the grace to overcome envy and jealousy when you learn the secret of Psalms 37:4, "Delight yourself in the Lord; and He will give you the desires of your heart" (NAS).

15

Loneliness

Monos, meaning single, or alone. Producing a sense of separation or alienation from others.

Loneliness is one of the most painful problems in life. You can be in a crowd and still feel all alone—alone with yourself, your fears, your problems, your needs. Hundreds are bustling around you, but still you feel unwanted, unneeded, unimportant. You think: *Nobody understands,* or worse, *Nobody cares!* Without a friend to share your burdens, life itself becomes futile, meaningless.

Life Is Meant to Be Shared

The Bible tells us that God was in perfect fellowship with Himself in eternity past (Genesis 1:26). Man was created to have fellowship with God (Genesis 2:7), yet God said: "It is not good that man should be alone . . ." (Genesis 2:18 NKJV). Therefore, God created woman to be a suitable helper or partner for man. They were to live in fellowship with each other and with God. However, the Bible also clearly indicates that God has called some to remain unmarried (Matthew 19:12). By itself, marriage is not the answer. Many married people are still lonely.

Position. If we are believers, our position in God's eyes never varies: "My sheep hear My voice, and I know them, and they follow Me; and I give eternal life to them, and they shall never perish; and no one shall snatch them out of My hand. My Father, who has given them to Me, is greater than all; and no one is able to snatch them out of the Father's hand" (John 10:27–29 NAS).

In Romans 8:35–39, we are told that nothing can separate us from Christ's love. Sometimes, though, a coolness creeps into our relationship with God. We feel distant, isolated from Him. Eventually we wonder, *Perhaps God doesn't love me anymore.* If this is so, then your problem is not one of position (that never varies), but relationship. Ask yourself how things stand between you and the Lord.

Purpose. A second need the soul has is that of purpose. Many people, especially those in their twenties, go through a time of confusion: They don't know who they are or where they're going. What they really have encountered is a crisis of purpose. Often they declare they can find little meaning to life. They turn to others, asking, "What's the true reason for living?" Quite likely, the Apostle Paul went through just such a stage in his younger days before he met Jesus Christ. In Philippians 3:8 (NAS), however, we see a man ardently pursuing the true goal of his life, "More than that, I count all things to be loss in view of the surpassing value of knowing Christ Jesus my Lord, for whom I have suffered the loss of all things, and count them but rubbish in order that I might gain Christ." Ask yourself what God's goal is for *your* life.

People.   God has created His children to have fellowship with one another. The Body of Christ serves many purposes, and one of the most important is to provide an avenue of support, encouragement, and emotional closeness. These are qualities that nourish the emotionally starved soul. If you are lonely, you owe it to yourself to step out and seek more contact with other human beings. Whether it is volunteering for a community project, taking an arts-and-crafts class, or joining a fellowship group at the church, interpersonal contact is a potent weapon against loneliness. "Two are better than one because they have a good return for their labor. For if either of them falls, the one will lift up his companion . . ." (Ecclesiastes 4:9, 10 NAS).

Pleasure.   One of the most common causes of loneliness is self-neglect, that is, neglecting our own soul's need for laughter and enjoyment. The Bible speaks often of the importance of laughter; loneliness and discouragement are seen as enemies of God's regenerative work within His people. Proverbs 13:12 (NAS) describes this need for enjoyment: "Hope deferred makes the heart sick, but desire fulfilled is a tree of life." Legitimate fun nourishes the soul. Just because society thinks you should spend your life on a lonely treadmill is no reason to believe God does. Get out there and find some things you really enjoy doing. Do them regularly, and take a friend along if you can.

Pause.   One little-known but very common cause of loneliness in the hectic, fast-paced world we live in comes, as it were, from avoiding one's own company.

Christ understood this well. At intervals, He withdrew to solitary spots to reexamine His life and commune with God. "And after He had sent the multitudes away, He went up to the mountain by Himself to pray; and when it was evening, He was there alone" (Matthew 14:23 NAS). For a Christian, times set aside for meditation and prayer are really indispensable. There is a certain nourishment which the soul requires that is only available in those quiet times of self-reflection and intimacy, which the Christian enjoys with God through the intercessory work of the Holy Spirit. One of the shortcomings of the modern-day Church is its lack of emphasis on personal worship and commune with God in the secret closets of our life. When this time of personal intimacy with God is in short supply, one of the symptoms the soul may manifest is an emotional sense of loneliness. The cure is to take a few hours during the next week for some real quality time in prayer and meditation with the Lord (*see* Matthew 6:6).

The Spirit of Comfort

Loneliness is a mental attitude. If we are living in fellowship with God, we are never really alone. He has promised never to leave us or forsake us (Hebrews 13:5). Just before His Ascension, Jesus declared, "Lo, I am with you alway, even unto the end of the world" (Matthew 28:20). This promise climaxes His Great Commission. He has sent us out to preach the Gospel to the entire world in the assurance of His continuing presence.

Over the centuries, that promise has sustained many a beleaguered saint. We never really face the problems of life alone, because Christ lives in us. He is ever present in the soul of the believer. Loneliness comes only when we lose sight of that truth. Christ promised: "I will not leave you comfortless ... I will send the Comforter ...

the Spirit of Truth ... which is the Holy Spirit" (John 14:18,16,17,26). Through the Spirit, we have peace and reassurance that Christ lives within us. A lonely Christian, therefore, is one who has forgotten who he is. He has forgotten that he is a child of the King, and instead begins to live like an emotional outcast. He has laid down his spiritual armor (Ephesians 6:10–18) and is wide open to attack. Forgetting his Lord's victory, he is already preparing for defeat. He is living as though God were dead!

Loneliness is a self-inflicted bitterness. It is the belief that God is not there and does not care about you. What really complicates this problem for the Christian is that he *knows* that is not true! He knows in his heart that he is not alone; he is indwelt by the Spirit of God. You are a "partaker of the divine nature" (2 Peter 1:4). Your life is coeternal with the life of God! When a Christian *feels* alone, it is because he is distracting himself from the source of all meaning and purpose in life—God, the Creator and Sustainer—our Companion.

No, Never Alone!

As a Christian, you are never really alone. Christ is always present in our lives through His indwelling Spirit. We *feel* alone when we see ourselves as victims of circumstance rather than victorious children of the living God.

Loneliness only comes when we fail to live in personal fellowship with Christ on a daily basis. If He is really alive and risen from the dead, why should you ever feel alone? Because your boyfriend dropped you? Because your husband died? Because your friend moved away? Because you lost your job? Never! The eternal God lives within you, and there is no excuse for loneliness!

You are a joint heir of Jesus Christ, who lives within you. You share in all that He is, all that He has. He has given you His righteousness and seated you with Him on His eternal throne! He has made you a child of God with an inheritance in heaven! He has done for you everything you could never have done for yourself!

God's continual daily presence in your soul will sustain you through all the hard times of life. You are not out there on the road of life pushing, shoving, and struggling to succeed all by yourself. The Christian life is far more than a struggle to survive; it is a dynamic and exciting daily personal encounter with the living God!

Even When We Sin, He Is There!

Even when we have sinned against God, David, the psalmist, reminds us that we are not permanently cut off from Him. In the face of his own sin, David cried, "Against thee, thee only, have I sinned" (Psalms 51:4). He was still painfully aware of the presence of God. In another place, he asks, "Whither shall I go from thy Spirit? or whither shall I flee from thy presence? If I ascend up into heaven, thou art there: if I make my bed in hell, behold, thou art there. If I take the wings of the morning, and dwell in the uttermost part of the sea; Even there shall thy hand lead me, and thy right hand shall hold me" (Psalms 139:7-10). God is everywhere, omnipresent. Thus, even in the depth of his worst sin, David stood in God's presence. Even in hell, there is a knowledge of the reality of the person of God.

Loneliness—that feeling of hopelessness and despair—is real. It has engulfed millions. Yet, for the Christian, there is no excuse for loneliness. Why?

- God is always there.
- Jesus promised never to leave or forsake us.

We are indwelt by the Holy Spirit of God and live in fellowship with Him.

- We are not cut off from God's purposes. We *are His purposes.*

He sent Christ to redeem us. He has commissioned us to take His Gospel to the entire world. We are not struggling to find a purpose in life. We know what that purpose is. Get out there! Start sharing the message, and you will never be lonely. Remember the Great Commission: "Go ye therefore, and teach all nations . . . and, lo, I am with you alway, even unto the end of the world. Amen" (Matthew 28:19, 20).

16

Pressure

Biazomai, *to be pressed, constrained.* **Kata-dunasteuomai,** *to be ruled, to be in subjection.*

No one can escape pressure; it affects everyone. Under pressure, one of two things always happens: We find ourselves strengthened and fortified from within (like a diamond), or we crack (like an egg). How we *handle* pressure will determine whether we stand or break.

Pressure begins in the mind. It is a result of how we think about ourselves and our responsibilities. Some people feel more pressure than others in the same situation because they look at life differently. People handle pressure differently. One may talk out his frustrations, while another finds relief only in pushing himself to his limits.

Causes of Pressure

The greatest cause of pressure is the individual himself. You pressure yourself by how you respond to the demands on your life. Therefore, learning to handle pressure involves learning how to deal with your attitude toward yourself.

1. Self-identity. Our own self-concept often makes us push ourselves. If you view yourself as superman or superwoman, your goal will be success at all costs. You will shrink from the slightest thought of failure. A poor self-concept, on the other hand, makes one dread even the smallest challenge.

2. Goals. Sometimes we suffer undue pressure because we set unrealistic goals for ourselves and then suffer agony when we fail to reach them. We become irritable and upset at the slightest obstacle. We need to turn these goals over to God. Surrender your plans to Him and make sure they are, in fact, *His* plans.

3. Fear. Fear is a major cause of stress. It distracts our gaze from the Almighty God and turns it onto our own scanty resources. Fear of failure in one situation actually causes greater fear in another. The more we fear, the more anxious we become, until we crack under pressure. Fear drives us away from people and responsibility. It is self-protecting and also self-destructive.

4. Time. One of the greatest pressures on busy people is a lack of time. Whenever you feel oppressed by a lack of time, you are trying to do too much! Today people accomplish more in one day than their ancestors did in a week, or even a month. The hurried pace of life nowadays makes us tackle more than we could possibly do. Age is also a factor. You may have been able to push yourself eighteen hours a day at age twenty-five, but at fifty, you may need to slow down.

5. Health. Many times we drive ourselves without making allowances for sickness. Have you ever felt you

simply had no time to be sick? Yet our ruthless pace
makes illness of some kind inevitable—laying us up, not
for days, but weeks and months. Health hazards are danger signals warning us to readjust our priorities.

6. Family. Family problems bring some of the
greatest pressures of all. Working men and women are
often under stress on the job because things are not
going well at home. Succeed at home, and you succeed
at work.

7. Finances. Financial mismanagement is a major
cause of pressure. It may leave you hopelessly in debt.
Certainly, it saps your mental and emotional strength. It
can only be corrected with time, trouble, and effort.

The Ultimate Cause: Irresponsibility

The ultimate cause of most pressure is irresponsibil-
ity. When we fail to manage our time, health, family,
and finances properly, we only add further pressure on
ourselves when that mismanagement catches up with us.
If you overschedule yourself on a given day, you will be
under pressure almost immediately and stay frustrated
all day long. If you don't take care of your health, you
will eventually break down physically.

Pressure is self-induced tension caused by irresponsible mismanagement. It can crush a person mentally and
emotionally. In the work place, middle managers are
most likely to crack under corporate pressure. The
bland, easygoing people seldom set records, but they survive because they pressure themselves so little. High-
performance people, on the other hand, often burn out.

The Inner Conflict: Sovereignty

The real inner conflict of self-induced pressure is our
struggle against God's sovereignty. We are actually at
war against His will for our lives. When we schedule
ourselves too tightly, or push ourselves too hard, we are

trying to do more than God really intends us to. All the pressure and conflict we suffer comes of seeking what we want, not what He wants.

Learning to accept our God-given limitations is just as important as learning to accept our God-given gifts and abilities. When we attempt to do more than God has planned for us, we will experience pressure. Therefore, learning to handle pressure means learning to accept God-given priorities and saying no to everything else.

Some Practical Suggestions

Wishing a problem would go away never makes it go away. Action is required on our part.

1. Surrender. Stop fighting God. Your agenda is not His agenda, if it is crushing you. While some pressure is normal in every situation, you cannot continually go from one pressure-packed situation to another without cracking. Surrender your goals to do His will.

2. Pray. Learn to release pressure through prayer. When you talk to God, you are talking to the sovereign Lord of the universe. True prayer will conquer worry and fear. Take your pressures to the Lord and get His direction.

3. Talk. Find someone who understands what you are going through; talk it out with him or her. While talking will not solve the problem, it will certainly release some of your tension. Do not be afraid to talk to your husband or wife, pastor, counselor, or friend.

4. Play. Some pressure can be released through physical recreation. Some people crack up because they get little or no physical exercise. Taking time to exercise will give you more quality time to work. Jog, hike, bowl, swim, bike, sail, write—whatever. Get out and go. You'll be glad you did.

5. Plan. Start planning your work and activities to

allow time for pressure release. Don't push yourself so hard or schedule yourself so full that you have no time to pray, meditate, or even reminisce. Leave yourself room to grow and develop as a human being.

Confronting Life's Crises

We hear much today about mid-life crisis. Our relentless pursuit of success and material prosperity has given us a burned-out society. Millions reach the age of forty and fifty and find themselves adrift, without purpose or direction. At this point, we are tempted to:

1. Go back—retreat to childhood or adolescence in search of peace and security. We find ourselves daydreaming, brooding about our "lost youth," wondering what might have been, and doubting our future.

2. Go under—collapse under the pressures of life. We cannot concentrate—our lives become aimless. Introspection, sudden emotional outbursts, and deep depression are symptoms. Drug use, alcoholism, and sexual infidelity are very common at this point as false "escape mechanisms" from the pressures of mid-life crisis.

What we really need to do in every crisis is *move ahead*. Face your pressure, reevaluate your priorities, reduce your agenda. Determine how much you can reasonably handle. Get a fresh start. Get out of your ruts and tackle something new. Recapture your full potential by doing a few things well, rather than a lot of things poorly. You still have great potential, but you can realize it only by doing what God has really called you to do.

17

Rejection

Atheteo, *to cast aside, refuse*. Similar to apodokimazo, *to reject as unfit or unworthy*.

People crave acceptance and fear rejection. Some seek acceptance in business, some in academics, some in athletics. Their key to acceptance is success, and they seek success by asserting themselves. Others seek acceptance through interpersonal relationships. Still others have given up looking. They settle for rejection. They reinforce that rejection through depressed behavior patterns such as alcohol or drug abuse.

The Pursuit of Acceptance

The lifelong pursuit of acceptance is deeply rooted in human personality. Many people are hungry and searching, without knowing the object of that search. First of all, man has an unquenchable desire to know his Creator. We are all driven by an innate desire for the spiritual and eternal realities of life. We need to know that God accepts us and that He will not reject us. That is why religion is central to man's understanding of himself. Only when you are convinced that God accepts you will you believe that others accept you, as well. Most of us fear rejection because we know just how sinful we really are. Acceptance from God thus becomes vital.

Second, man has an innate fear of rejection. Just as the human body has developed immunologic defense systems to resist infectious diseases, so, too, our personality is skilled at avoiding rejection. Overt rejection we can sidestep or evade, but subtler forms of rejection get past our defenses and leave deeper wounds. No one, for instance, expects to be loved by his enemies. It hurts most when a friend turns on us!

The Rejection Syndrome

A life pattern of rejection from early childhood onward can produce rejection syndrome. We become so used to rejection that after a while, we start bringing it on ourselves. Many things can bring on rejection syndrome:

1. Conditional (performance-based) love. Some children unconsciously believe they are loved only when they succeed—when they do well in school, sports, music, and so forth.

2. Unfavorable comparison. When parents seem to favor one child, the other will feel neglected. While sibling rivalries are normal, selective praise and unfavorable comparison all breed feelings of rejection. No two children are exactly alike in their abilities and interests; comparisons are unfair and unhealthy.

3. Deprivation of parental love. Prolonged illness, hospital stays, military service—any of these can separate parents from their children for long periods of time. Consequently, some children come to feel themselves unloved, uncared for. In such cases, a loving parent will do all he or she can to reassure the child.

4. Divorce. All children are vulnerable to the tragedy of divorce. Preteens especially tend to blame themselves unjustly, feeling their own worth as a human being has been called into question by the divorce.

5. Overprotection. Smothering a child will leave him stifled and unfulfilled. Although usually done with good intentions, overprotective parenting develops unhealthy fears in children. They dread leaving the nest when they grow up.

6. "Refrigerator" parents. Some parents genuinely love their children but cannot express that love verbally or physically. Such coldness will leave the children feeling rejected, perhaps ultimately incapable of expressing love themselves.

7. Child abuse. The ultimate form of rejection is mental or physical abuse. The unwanted child detects his parents' rejection easily, as do some handicapped children.

8. Teenage rejection. The adolescent is the most vulnerable to social rejection. Teens who feel rejected by their peers form personality patterns that often last a lifetime. Their fear of rejection makes them either blind conformists or willful eccentrics.

9. Young-adult insecurity. Rejected teens grow up to be insecure young adults. They usually have trouble making friends with the opposite sex. Their closest friends also tend to be social outcasts. Their fear of rejection often spurs them to bizarre behavior that only brings further rejection.

10. Adult dysfunction. When adolescents and

young adults fail to find security and acceptance, their personality failings as adults become glaringly obvious. They are prone to failure both at home and at work, which only deepens their sense of not belonging.

Acceptance Begins With God

Hell is the ultimate rejection—perpetual exclusion from God's presence. Yet God does not want to reject people. To avert that punishment, He poured out His wrath on His Son. He nailed our sins to His Cross. The penalty has been paid; no barriers stand between us and God. Evil and thankless as we are, He offers us His love and acceptance.

The Scripture tells us the believer is an adopted and accepted child of God (Ephesians 1:5, 6). We are "accepted in the beloved." Christ is in God, and we are in Christ. Thus, through our spiritual union with Him, we are secure. Our acceptance is based not on performance, but on our relationship with Him. Since the Father is satisfied with Christ's sacrifice for our sins, He accepts us totally as His children. Because of His atonement on the Cross, our debt is canceled and we are new creations in Christ Jesus (2 Corinthians 5:17).

Overcoming Rejection

While our experiences during childhood may have ingrained in us a pattern of rejection, that pattern can be broken. No one need remain a victim of his past. Four steps are necessary:

1. Accept God's love. Stop running from the God who loves you. Accept His forgiveness; claim His acceptance!

2. Stop rejecting yourself. In Christ you are a child of God. Stop denying your sonship. You are a joint heir with Jesus. Act like it! Self-rejection denies your new identity in Christ.

3. Stop blaming others.   While other people may have rejected you, they are not your real problem—you are! Rejection is an attitude within ourselves. Stop blaming your condition on everybody else.

4. Start living like a child of the King.   "... him that cometh to me," says Christ, "I will in no wise cast out" (John 6:37). You are *accepted* by God in Christ; your sins are covered. You are a member of God's family. *Stop complaining!*

Suffering

Pascho, to suffer in mind or body. Often used in combination with several words specifying to suffer ... long ... loss ... need ... persecution ... shame.

The Bible makes it clear that it is not always God's will to heal our infirmities. Rather, the Scripture emphatically states that God uses suffering to develop qualities in our lives we never had. The Apostle Paul was familiar with suffering and grief. In 2 Corinthians 1:3, 4, he refers to the Lord as the "God of all comfort; Who comforteth us in all our tribulation, that we may be able to comfort them which are in any trouble. . . ." Here we see a purpose behind suffering—helping others.

Suffering Has Meaning

In God's dealings with His children, no suffering is meaningless. For the Christian believer, ". . . all things work together for good to them that love God, to them who are the called according to his purpose" (Romans 8:28). In order to fully accept our circumstances and gain victory over each discouragement, the Christian must always believe that God is greater than his or her circumstances. There is no problem too big for God. When we become too problem conscious, we cease to be Christ-conscious. When we feel overwhelmed by our problems, we are actually doubting the purpose and character of God. Our discouragement and frustration illustrate our belief that God has failed us. In reality, He is always working *for* us (Romans 8:31).

Even the greatest of human tragedies can accomplish invaluable good, when we view it in the light of eternity. Our shortsighted temporal viewpoint often blinds us to God's great purposes. The death of Jesus Christ seemed to be a mistake, until His resurrection. Death is never a tragedy for the child of God. The Bible tells us, "Precious in the sight of the Lord is the death of his saints" (Psalms 116:15).

Several years ago, at the funeral of a dear godly woman who had died after many years of physical suffering, many people questioned God's wisdom in allowing such a good woman to suffer so much. Through all her suffering, her confidence in God's love had never wavered. At her funeral, the minister read the text: "For I reckon that the sufferings of this present time are not worthy to be compared with the glory which shall be revealed in us" (Romans 8:18).

As the years rolled by, God used her unwavering testimony to impress upon her children and grandchildren the importance of devotion to Christ. Each time one of them was tempted to turn away from the will of God, he was drawn back by the remembrance of her life and testimony. In a very real sense, she "being dead, yet speaketh!"

Why Do Christians Suffer?

Sometimes suffering is the consequence of sinful disobedience. Sometimes we suffer because we deserve to suffer for our wrong actions. However, this is only one cause of suffering. While Acts 5:3–11 and 1 Corinthians 11:28–31 make it clear that believers may suffer for wrongdoing, the Bible also emphatically states that all suffering is not the result of sin. Job suffered greatly, not because of sin, but as a lesson to Satan and his friends! Paul was severely beaten, stoned, and shipwrecked for the cause of the Gospel. Throughout Church history, many great saints of God have suffered persecution so the Church might grow. Missionaries have given their very lives to bring the Gospel to the remote regions of the earth. It is quite obvious that all suffering is not an act of judgment against sin. There are many "causes" of suffering, but all of them are under the control of God. Remember, Satan could not touch Job without God's permission (Job 1:12; 2:6). Suffering has many purposes:

"Cause" of suffering	Purpose of suffering	Scripture
Sin	To warn us of the consequences of sin	1 Corinthians 11:28–31
Conformity	To conform us in our weakness to Christ's image (His personality)	Romans 12:1, 2; 1 Peter 4:12, 13
Commitment	To develop deep spiritual qualities in our lives through perseverance	Romans 5:3
Compassion	To enable us to identify with and help others	2 Corinthians 1:4
Encouragement	To testify to those whose faith is weak	2 Corinthians 1:6
Evangelism	To convince the unsaved that God's grace is real	2 Corinthians 4:11; 2 Corinthians 6:3–5

God's Sovereign Purposes

As human beings, we tend to view every circumstance of life from a selfish and temporal vantage point. Our heavenly Father, however, operates from a divine eternal perspective. He sees the consequences of a given event, far into the future.

We have all heard stories of the miraculous deliverance of believers from danger. Yet we must not forget those who were not delivered. Millions have suffered death for the cause of Christ over the centuries. Why does God spare some and not others?

Our final answer must lie in God's sovereign purposes. No one deliberately chooses to suffer. We cannot understand the timing and purpose of God adequately to ask to suffer at our convenience. Yet God permits suffering to come into our lives just when we need it most. He reminds us: "Yea, and all that will live godly in Christ Jesus shall suffer persecution" (2 Timothy 3:12). Paul prayed that the Corinthian church would learn how to suffer: "And our hope of you is stedfast, knowing, that as ye are partakers of the sufferings, so shall ye be also of the consolation (2 Corinthians 1:7).

God's Sufficient Grace

The Apostle Paul had a problem. In 2 Corinthians 12:7-9, he says: ". . . there was given to me a thorn in the flesh . . . For this thing I besought the Lord thrice, that it might depart from me. And he said unto me, 'My grace is sufficient for thee: for my strength is made perfect in weakness. . . .' " In his case, God chose to glorify Himself by leaving the affliction, not by removing it.

We all praise God for His miraculous sparing of evangelist Charles Hughes' life. All would agree that He had a purpose in Charles's accident. But we are equally convinced that God's purpose has been accomplished in the loss of some of our students who have died in accidents. In either case, whether in life or death, God has been glorified. Confronted with pain or tragedy, we must ever turn our faces heavenward and receive God's all-sufficient grace. For the Christian, life is never lost; it is invested in eternity. "For I reckon that the sufferings of this present time are not worthy to be compared with the glory which shall be revealed in us" (Romans 8:18).

Three Steps to Dealing With Adversity: Y.E.S.

- Yield to God's purposes in the matter.
- Eliminate false ideas about suffering.
- Surrender to a plan of action.

1. Yield to God's purposes and seek His wisdom.

Whenever adversity comes into the life of the Christian, it comes with one of three purposes:

- Temptations—to bring you down (from Satan)
- Tests—to bring you through (from the world)
- Tribulations—to bring you up (from God)

Any adversity that comes into our lives is one of these three. Satan, of course, wants to destroy us and blot out our Christian testimony. Tests and trials, on the other hand, are inevitable consequences of a fallen world. Every day, Christians and non-Christians alike undergo tests of endurance and trials of patience, but only the Christian can rest assured that trials and calamities are God's tool to perfect the character of His children. Certain tribulations and afflictions in our lives are initiated by the Lord. These are targeted for the development of specific character qualities of Christlikeness and holiness within us, which could not be accomplished by other means. The chart on page 141 compares and contrasts these three different sources of adversity and suffering.

2. Eliminate misconceptions about suffering.

• Misconception number 1: When you have problems, it means you are not spiritual. An examination of the Bible quickly reveals that God's closest friends often have the hardest times. Adversity is often God's tool to perfect the believer's character.

Category	Source	Affliction	References	Purpose
Temptation	Satan	*Peirasmos,* an intentional event designed to overcome or destroy.	1 Corinthians 10:13	To *eradicate* the believer's fellowship with God.
Tribulations	The World	*Thlipis,* a pressure surrounding the Christian. *Pathema,* a pressure arising within the Christian. *Kakoucheo,* a pressure directed at the Christian from without.	1 Peter 4:12 1 Peter 1:7	To *improve* the believer's ability to withstand setbacks and overcome obstacles.
Tests	God	*Purosis,* trial by fire.	2 Thessalonians 1:4; 2 Corinthians 1:5; Hebrews 13:3	To *inbuild* more of the character of Christ within the believer.

• Misconception number 2:   Reading the Bible will automatically solve all your problems. To read the Word, or hear it preached, is not the same as to *obey* the Word. Prayer and perseverance are needed to make the Word come alive in our lives. Here we need the Spirit's work as we read and ponder the Scriptures.

• Misconception number 3:   The answers to all of the problems you will face are explicitly found in the Bible. The Bible is God's inerrant Word, but it has little to say about changing spark plugs or finding your way through downtown Chicago. The Bible focuses on the larger issues of life—man's character and obligations. Tackle these issues, and you will find yourself better able to handle the smaller problems.

• Misconception number 4:   Because you are a Christian, you will not have any problems. This may seem like a ridiculous statement, but, unfortunately, it is the unspoken expectation of many Christians. Christ says in John 10:10, "I am come that they might have life, and that they might have it more abundantly." He is not implying that God issues an invincible suit of armor to each new Christian at the time of conversion. He is promising abundance in life, sometimes through adversity and sometimes through enjoyment, but always with the manifest purpose of conforming our character to that of Jesus Christ. The Bible tells us that the rains fall both on the good men and the evil men of this world, and so, too, the problems of being human befall Christians as well as non-Christians.

3. Surrender to a plan of action.

• Expand your lines of communication with the Lord. We all, as Christians, have a certain level of communication with God. During times of adversity, we need to increase the intensity of our communication with Him through intensified Bible study, Scripture memory, meditation, and prayer.

• Limit your vulnerability. A time of adversity is probably not a time to take on more responsibilities. Use that time to consolidate your position spiritually. Try to discern God's will for you.

• Limit exaggeration and overstatement. Taking office amid the Great Depression, President Roosevelt declared, "The only thing we have to fear is fear itself." Oftentimes Christians panic during times of trouble and make hasty decisions. God tells us in His Word to, "be still and know that I am God." Stop, look, and pray is sound advice. In times of trouble, keep your head.

• Watch what you say. There is little to be gained by spreading your problem to everyone in your church, your neighborhood, and your community. It is more common for God to work in the quiet of your own heart, in conjunction with the prayers of a few trusted Christians. Do not share too much, too soon, with too many people—let God work discreetly.

• Seek wise counsel. The Bible, especially Proverbs, urges the Christian to seek counsel from godly men and women. The same Holy Spirit dwells in all Christians, and the wisdom brought to you by a brother or sister in Christ may well come from Him. But choose your counselors wisely. Consider their lives: Do they know the Lord? Are they walking with Him?

• Be teachable. Christians suffer needlessly when they refuse to learn the first time. The Scriptures teach that God opposes the proud and obstinate. Learn from the circumstances God put you in. Don't make Him repeat the lesson over and over.

• In any situation, resolve to achieve whatever goal God has set you. God seldom hurries. The children of Israel waited four hundred years before God sent them a deliverer. We Christians must likewise be prepared to wait. God will work His purposes through our lives to our ultimate good, "Being confident of this very thing, that he which hath begun a good work in you will perform it until the day of Christ Jesus" (Philippians 1:6).

Temptation

Peirasmos, *meaning a trial or temptation.*

Ever since the days of Adam and Eve, man has been tempted. The Bible reminds us, "There hath no temptation taken you but such as is common to man ..." (1 Corinthians 10:13). Your battle with temptation is not unique to you. It is a universal problem.

But Scripture also reminds us that "every man is tempted, when he is drawn away of his own lust, and enticed" (James 1:14).

One of the major reasons people cannot handle the problem of temptation is their refusal to face the real source of their temptation: themselves! We must face the fact that we are our own worst enemies. The real source of temptation is neither God nor Satan. In most cases, temptation begins in one's own heart as he is "drawn away of his own lust." All too often, the Christian believer refuses to admit to himself that he is toying with sin—until it is too late.

Don't Blame the Devil

The easiest way to avoid any personal responsibility regarding our own sin is to blame it on the devil. Many people claim that they cannot deal with their temptation because "the devil made me do it."

One well-meaning lady told her counselor that she really didn't yell and scream at her husband. "The devil makes me do it," she insisted.

Her counselor replied, "I can't make the devil stop yelling at your husband, but I can make *you* stop."

Remember, Satan is not omnipresent; he is a limited, created being. Chances are that Satan has never dealt with you personally. Also, a born-again Christian is no longer under Satan's control. While he may trouble you from without (and that only by God's permission—*see* Job 1:12), he no longer has a claim over your life. His power has been broken by the victorious death and resurrection of Christ. Try as he might, Satan cannot enter your mind and possess your will, thoughts, or emotions.

It took nearly twenty minutes to convince this housewife that she was indeed responsible for yelling at her husband. Finally she burst into tears: "You're right, I did it! I yelled at him myself!"

"Good!" the counselor replied. "You see, we can stop your husband from aggravating you, and we can get you to stop yelling at him, but we can't make the devil stop!"

Don't Blame God

In the depth of our frustration with temptation, we may even be tempted to blame God for our problems.

You may ask yourself, *Why is God doing this to me?* However, the Bible clearly teaches that God is not the author of temptation. "Let no man say when he is tempted, I am tempted of God: for God cannot be tempted with evil, neither tempteth he any man" (James 1:13).

God may allow Satan to tempt us, but even then, the Bible promises ". . . God is faithful, who will not suffer you to be tempted above that ye are able . . ." (1 Corinthians 10:13). There is no excuse, then, for failure or defeat. Should I fail, I have only myself to blame. If God let temptation come to men such as Abraham, Job, Moses, David, and Paul, why should I expect to be exempt?

The Battle Begins in Your Mind

The Bible tells us plainly that what we think (*logizomai*) not only determines how we live, but reflects who we are. "For as [a man] thinketh in his heart, so is he" (Proverbs 23:7). Every Christian knows what it is to be enslaved to lust or hatred. Greed, jealousy, envy—all these are poison to the soul. Recognizing this, the Apostle Paul wrote:

> Finally, brethren, whatsoever things are true, whatsoever things are honest, whatsoever things are just, whatsoever things are pure, whatsoever things are lovely, whatsoever things are of good report; if there be any virtue, and if there be any praise, think on these things.
>
> Philippians 4:8

Seven steps will help the Christian clean up his or her thought life:

1. Admit that you have a problem. Rationalizing sin will never cure it. Whatever sinful thoughts we are troubled with, we must confess them to God. Be honest with Him who searches our hearts and minds and knows our thoughts. Read 2 Samuel 12 or Psalms 51—and learn the importance of laying your sin before God.

2. *Believe that God can make a difference in your thought life.* There are no doubting victorious Christians. In Hebrews 11:6, we learn that without faith, we cannot please God; if we are to approach Him for strength or wisdom, we must believe Him capable of supplying it. "Blessed be the Lord, who daily bears our burden, The God who is our salvation. God is to us a God of deliverances . . ." (Psalms 68:19, 20 NAS).

3. *Take a long, hard look at yourself.* God gives no blessing to Christians that hold out on Him. "If I regard wickedness in my heart, The Lord will not hear" (Psalms 66:18 NAS). If our minds are to be renewed, we must be painfully honest—both with God and ourselves. Search out and confess those thoughts that displease Him.

4. *Make a 100 percent commitment.* There must come a point when we are revolted at our own vileness. It is at this point God wants the Christian to resolve to, "go all the way with God's way." This means conforming every thought to the holiness enjoined in Scripture. David put it this way:

> Thy word is a lamp to my feet, And a light to my path. I have sworn, and I will confirm it, That I will keep Thy righteous ordinances. . . . I have inclined my heart to perform Thy statutes Forever, *even* to the end.
>
> Psalms 119:105, 106, 112 (NAS)

5. *Be flexible and willing to change.* Jesus likened a stagnant Christian to an old wineskin—no longer flexible, incapable of holding new wine. Christians who have become narrow-minded, stale, and complacent are especially vulnerable to un-Christlike thoughts. These we must set aside. God's goal for us is the perfect holiness exemplified in His Son.

6. See God as the only refuge. We live in a society geared to human pride and self-sufficiency. Even Christians sometimes forget that only God is our true deliverer. David acknowledged as much: "O give us help against the adversary, For deliverance by man is in vain" (Psalms 60:11 NAS). Or again:

> Through God we shall do valiantly, And it is He who will tread down our adversaries. . . . Trust in Him at all times, O people; Pour out your heart before Him; God is a refuge for us.
> Psalms 60:12; 62:8 (NAS)

7. Renewal is a full-time job. Romans 12:2 teaches that we are "transformed by the renewing of our minds." But we must be vigilant. A daily quiet time in the Word is essential. Are you often troubled by an unclean thought? Find the appropriate Scripture and quote it to yourself when that thought comes around again. Start memorizing Scripture—maybe three or four verses every week. Learn to meditate on Scripture, asking the Holy Spirit for aid and illumination. Ask God to reveal His attributes to you. Seek to know Him in every thought and deed.

Follow through on these seven steps, and you will find your thinking more and more Christlike. Your soul is at stake here. You can choose either to cleanse your mind with God's Holy Word, or surrender it to unclean thoughts prompted by Satan, God's adversary and ours.

Take Definite and Immediate Steps of Action

Read 1 Corinthians 10:13. The chapter opens by reminding us how the Israelites were tempted in the wilderness. God was not pleased with them, and they were "overthrown in the wilderness" (v. 5). The Apostle Paul then goes on.

These things, he says, happened for our example (vv. 6-10). We should take warning and not:

- *Lust*
- *Be idolaters*
- *Commit fornication*
- *Tempt Christ*
- *Murmur*

The first step in conquering temptation is to visualize the sin and its terrible consequences. All too often, we try to rationalize away the seriousness of sin and thereby fall victim to its clutches. Sin is no laughing matter with God. It is rebellious disobedience to His Law. However, you do not need to fall into sin if you will follow God's prescription for conquering temptation.

1. Admit to yourself that you are being tempted. Acknowledge your own feelings. Face your temptation head-on and determine to *do* something about it!

2. Confess to God that you are tempted to sin. We are not only to confess our sins to God, but even the very fact that we *desire* to sin. Remember that God sees everything you are doing, and He knows everything you are thinking (*see* Psalms 139:2). Run to Him in prayer and ask for His help now, before you sin.

3. Seek the help of a Christian friend. Two kinds of friends are to be avoided: the harsh, censorious type and the overlenient type. Go to someone who will help you turn from sin without turning from you. Ask to pray with that person. The Bible reminds us that we are to "bear . . . one another's burdens, and so fulfill the law of Christ (Galatians 6:2).

4. Remember—no excuses for failure. "There

hath no temptation taken you but such as is common to man" (1 Corinthians 10:13). Others have won out over temptation; why should you be an exception? Sin is sin. Stop thinking about what to do, or why you are feeling overwhelmed, and decide to do what you know to be right! "Resist the devil, and he will flee from you" (James 4:7).

5. Trust God to give you the victory. He is faithful! If you really believe that, you will deal with your temptation by making "no provision for the flesh." You cannot expect God to help you when, at the same time, you are preparing to disobey Him.

6. Take the "way of escape!" Get away from the source of your temptation. If you are tempted to smoke or drink or look at dirty magazines, don't stand around drugstores or liquor stores. Learn to say no.

20

Worry

Merimna, *meaning a care, anxious thought.*

Worry is practically an epidemic in our affluent society. The medical word for worry is *anxiety,* and every year, Americans spend millions of dollars on tranquilizers and nerve relaxers to conquer anxiety. Christians get especially frustrated over worry, because they know they are not supposed to worry. So they worry about worrying!

Worry Is a Sin

Worry is anxiety over circumstances beyond our control. The worrier really believes that the world ought to revolve around him and that nothing should ever happen against his will or plans. Worry stems from selfishness and from an inability to trust the sovereignty of God: "All things work together for good to them that love God, to them who are the called according to his purpose" (Romans 8:28).

The Bible clearly teaches us not to worry: "Be anxious for nothing . . ." (Philippians 4:6 NAS). The Authorized Version says: "Be careful for nothing," meaning "full of care" (or worry). Sometimes, we pray that our worries will go away, but they never do. How can we deal with the problem of worry?

Worry Is Not Fear

First, we should get straight the distinction between worry and fear. Fear is a natural and healthy response to danger. Fear of pain keeps children from touching a hot stove; fear of falling makes an adult hang on when fixing the roof. For our own protection, God gave us a capacity to be afraid.

Anxiety (worry), on the other hand, is formless. Nothing concrete brings on the dread. For the most part, we should listen to our fears but cast a critical eye on worry and anxiety. The following chart compares the two.

Fear	Anxiety
1. Comes and goes quickly.	1. Lingers. If anything, it gets worse with time.
2. Usually triggered by a clear-cut threat from without.	2. Usually originates within ourselves. Often we cannot tell what caused it.
3. Specific.	3. Vague, ill-defined.
4. Sharpens the senses. We feel alert, quick to respond.	4. Paralyzing. We dither and hesitate.
5. We focus on the danger from without.	5. The feeling itself is dominant. We grope at random, unfocused.

6. Free of inner conflict.

7. Goes away when the threat is averted.

6. Often generates inner conflict. Our thinking is jerky, indecisive.

7. Causes erratic, disturbed behavior. Lingers even when things seem to get better.

God's Plan to Conquer Worry

Philippians 4:4–9 gives us five specific steps for conquering the problem of worry. We must follow all five, which are in the form of commands in the original text.

1. "Rejoice in the Lord alway" (v. 4). The Lord that redeemed us is the Lord of circumstances. Nothing can possibly happen that God cannot turn to our benefit. The command to rejoice is based on the fact that our rejoicing is *in* the Lord. True joy is not dependent upon our circumstances but upon our confidence that God is in control of those circumstances. Thus, we can learn to rejoice *always.*

2. "Let your moderation be known unto all men" (v. 5). The word *moderation* means reasonable, temperate, or appropriate and implies yieldedness to God. The believer lives a moderate life-style because he is yielded to the control of the Holy Spirit. The degree of our inward yieldedness will determine the degree of outward moderation. Yielding to the Lordship of Christ brings consolation in place of conflict and confidence instead of capitulation. Many Christians worry because they are not presently yielding control of their lives to the authority of Christ. They know Him as Savior and have acknowledged His Lordship, but in their moment of anxiety, they are not consciously trusting in and yielding to His authority.

3. Do not worry—pray! (vv. 6, 7.) The third step is the most difficult of all, because it sounds so simple:

Don't worry, pray! "But I've *tried* that," people often say. Now, one of two things is true: Either they have genuinely sought God in prayer and the Bible is untrue, or the Bible remains true but something was lacking in their prayer.

There can be no doubt that the biblical antidote for worry is prayer: ". . . but in every thing by prayer and supplication with thanksgiving let your requests be made known unto God. And the peace of God . . . shall keep your hearts and minds . . ." (vv. 6, 7). Several things should be observed about this command. Prayer includes both the worship of praise and the petition of requests. It must be rendered in everything (all of life's circumstances). Requests must be made with thanksgiving, trusting God by faith for His answer. Having really prayed, the believer must have the confidence that his needs have been made known to God. Worry denies the reality of prayer. Worriers do not really pray. They may utter their anxieties and frustrations before God, but they do not really pray in faith with thanksgiving, or else they would receive the result of true praying: the peace of God.

4. Learn to think right (v. 8). Wrong thinking is the real cause of worry. Notice that the text does not stop by telling us not to worry, but goes on to tell us how not to worry by learning to do right thinking. Verse 8 commands us to think on these things: that which is true, honest, just, pure, lovely, admirable, virtuous, and praiseworthy. While it is true that the power of positive thinking has been overemphasized by some, it is also true that its value has been greatly neglected by many others. Right thinking is the basis of right living.

If worry (anxiety) is unfounded fear, then in your thinking choose which of the following five methods you will use to deal with your fear:

A. *Curse* the presence of fear and anxiety. This may

appear to help in the short run, but eventually produces anger and resentment toward God.

B. *Nurse* the fear. This will in time produce self-pity.

C. *Rehearse* the fear and anxiety. This will cause you to actually cling to your worries and anxiety in an unconscious attempt to manipulate others or gather subtle sympathy from them.

D. *Disperse* the fear and worry. This causes "dumping" of problems on others or taking out your frustrations on them, which can lead to self-denial and self-deception concerning the real causes of your problems.

E. *Reverse* the fear and anxiety patterns in your thinking. Choose to see your problems as *projects* God can use in working out His eventual good in your life. For each disability we fear we have, He has a matching ability that He will use in our behalf. There are always hidden possibilities in every circumstance when we're trusting in God and when we refuse to quit. Living by faith and expecting God's blessings in spite of the problems will tap His provision in the situation.

Worry comes of dwelling on ourselves and our problems, not on God and His solutions. Christians need to be Christ-centered, not problem centered. Teach yourself to meditate on wholesome things. Replace negative anxieties with positive truths. Don't surrender control of your life to a problem; give it over to the Holy Spirit, who can solve the problem.

5. *Learn to live right* (v. 9). Verse 9 tells us that what we have learned, and received, and heard, and seen by example, we must now *do,* that is, practice (Greek present tense, with continuing action). *Do* the truth, and you will conquer worry. Think and act like a Christian with an unshakable trust in Christ's absolute Lordship. Only then can you rejoice in all things, live a yielded life, pray with faith, and think wholesome thoughts.

Spiritual Maturity

Spiritual maturity is the antidote to worry (spiritual bondage). But no Christian matures overnight. Don't be discouraged if you are not yet what you want to be and can be in Christ. Keep on practicing the Christian lifestyle. As you mature, true Christian conduct will become second nature to you. You will find yourself trusting God more and worrying less.

When we learn the discipline of Christian living, we have the assurance that the God of peace shall be with us (v. 9). Note the progression in our relationship with God. At salvation, we have "peace with God." When we learn to overcome worry with prayer, we have "the peace of God." Finally, in maturity, we find the very "God of peace" dwelling with us. We learn to value this presence even above His blessings. Only then do we find this peace "keeping [lit. "standing guard over"] our hearts and minds through Christ Jesus" (v. 7).

Conclusion

Life is a pilgrimage. It is a process of growth. There are no shortcuts to maturity. You can get there only by walking the rough road of life, no matter what obstacles may lie in your way. But it is in that process that we learn to deal with the problems of life. For problems are meant to make us better, not bitter. They are divinely appointed opportunities to bring us to spiritual maturity.

Thus, it is that we are pilgrims on the road of life. Never content with the temporal, we press on to the eternal. Never defeated by our failures, we recognize that our victory is in Christ. Therefore, we can face any problem of life, knowing that we are in His love and care.

In *Pilgrim's Progress,* John Bunyan wrote:

> Where am I now? In this love and care
> Of Jesus for the men that pilgrims are?
> Thus to provide that I should be forgiven!
> And dwell already the next door to heaven!

Whatever your problems may be, they pale into insignificance in the light of eternity. No matter how great your failures, God's grace is greater still. Lift up your heart and face life head-on. Do not avoid your problems. Tackle each one directly, knowing that God will help you through. The tougher the problem, the greater His grace will be.

Remember, no one is up all the time. When we are on top of things, we need to pull up those who are down, so that when we are down they can pull us up. That is what the family of God is all about. Each one ministers to the other so that all are helped. You will never be totally successful all the time. But you can learn from your mistakes.

Never give up! The last hill always seems like the toughest. Life is a marathon, not a hundred-yard dash. You can't win the race in the first lap. You have to keep running until you're finally home. Pace yourself. Be prepared for the detours and trouble spots. When they come along, don't give up the race. Remember, when the going gets tough, the tough get going.

God understands your struggle. He designed the trouble spots to toughen us and to mature us for the final lap. He also knows how much you can take. He will never put more on you than He has put within you to meet the challenge. When the race is run and your goal is reached, you will be able to say with the Apostle Paul: "For I reckon that the sufferings of this present time are not worthy to be compared with the glory which shall be revealed in us" (Romans 8:18).

May God grant you grace for the journey.